WHO AM I?

A Scientific Perspective

Time is like a river. You cannot touch the same water twice because the flow that has passed will never pass again. Enjoy every moment of life.

– Lao Tzu

Dr Vidyasagar Abburi

PARTRIDGE
A Penguin Random House Company

To order additional copies of this book, contact
Partridge India
000 800 10062 62
orders.india@partridgepublishing.com

www.partridgepublishing.com/india

Contents

Dedication   v

Acknowledgement   vii

Preface   ix

Chapter One
You and me are a miracle!   1

Chapter Two
The first miracle: The Universe itself and our
planet Earth which sustains life   11

Chapter Three
The second miracle: Evolution of life from microbes to humans   25

Chapter Four
The third miracle: The incredible cell which keeps you alive   37

Chapter Five
The fourth miracle: All life is one and yet you are unique   49

Chapter Six
The fifth miracle: Your body and brain   61

Chapter Seven
The flow of life   75

Appendix   84

Appendix A: Metabolism   85

Appendix B: Homeostasis   87

Appendix C: Hormones   90

Appendix D: Proteins and Enzymes   93

Appendix E: Neurons   99

Inspired By   106

Bibliography   108

Glossary   110

Dedication

This book is dedicated to my mother Late Lakshmikantham Abburi who lived her life with love, compassion and goodwill for all beings. She remains a source of inspiration to pursue goals that leave the world a better place to live than what we inherited.

Acknowledgement

I would like to acknowledge our entire team at *wonderwhizkids* for their efforts in making the book more engaging and interesting. I would like to thank Ms. Sirisha Kandukuri, Ms. Pushpa Bharathi Kurra, Mr. Ramesh Kosaraju and Mr. S. Venkata Nagan for sharing their ideas, knowledge and experience and also for encouraging me to complete the initiative of publishing this book. I would like to thank Partridge Publishing for helping me out to get my book published.

Look deep into nature, and then you will understand everything better. – Albert Einstein

Preface

The fundamental question that is sure to confront or puzzle all of us at some time or other is –"who am I?" The best minds in the categories of philosophers, spiritualists, scientists, theologians including people from all walks of life have discussed and debated the topic stimulating our imaginations. Note a profound paradox: "If TRUTH is universal", why so many doctrines about it? Perhaps the 'smiling silence' of the 'Enlightened' for the many teasing queries of disciples is indicative. Truth is a perception in the path of self-discovery, unique and distinct to individuals embracing the specific choice of the paradigm.

The book is an attempt to give an overview of the most likely answers to the questions we keep asking ourselves: Who am I? What is life? How did we come to exist? How do you become you? And how trillions and trillions of events happened exactly the way they should for you to be reading this book right now. The likely answers to these questions are explained by way of five miracles: the Universe itself and planet Earth which is right for life to evolve; evolution of life from microbes to humans; the incredible cell which is the basic unit of life; the uniqueness of each one of us; and finally our body and brain. The word "miracle" used in this book does not represent anything which is considered supernatural but represents extraordinary nature of "Nature". The planet Earth itself is a tiny speck in the visible Universe with ten billion large galaxies and 2000 billion billion Suns. We are such a small part in the Universe but every one of us is a Universe of small things miraculously working together to keep us alive. There are trillions of cells in you and me with hundred million neurons making something like 100 trillion neural connections, right now, in every one of us while you read this. The so called five miracles explained in this book are only a tip of the iceberg and would only help us as a pointer rather than presenting the truth in its entirety. The Chinese proverb, "you can't fill a bottomless cup or a filled cup", prods the seeker of truth to be receptive and shun prejudice.

This book presents a world view based on scientific discoveries as of now, which is bound to be modified by findings in future as we gain more insights about the true nature of "Nature". The scientific world view is more objective and rational without demanding any commitment from us to believe anything in particular. We marvel and wonder at the way fireflies light up a summer evening; or like a way chicken is born from an egg; the colors and smells of nature which bring subtle messages of infinite variety; and all of them arise out of trillions of transformations at the molecular level. The key messages you may like to reflect upon are the infinite possibilities of randomness in nature and how everything seem to have worked out very well even though odds are very high.

The understanding we gain from probing and reflecting on the truth about who we are suggests that there are an infinite variety of ever changing and yet repetitive patterns in the flow of energy as waves and particles within the framework of our body and mind. The flow of thoughts, emotions and feelings is represented by incessant flow of molecules, atoms and subatomic particles in countless ways. The scientific perspective enables understanding of our true nature as a flow of energy with connections to the cosmos at atomic as well as subatomic level. It suggests that I, the consciousness is an integral, inseparable part of the flow of life which is changing every moment in infinite ways.

The experience of self as a flow, experienced through the practice of "mindfulness" could also lead to the insight that everything including the self is impermanent. If we are constantly aware of what is going on in our body and mind by recognizing infinite variety of subtle changes in the flow of life occurring at every moment, we are likely to gain freedom from the delusion of self as something eternal, residing in us. The author is of the opinion that understanding of self as a miracle in the flow of life helps us develop gratitude which leads to happiness arising out of love and compassion for all beings and the feeling of 'Oneness' with 'Nature'.

Chapter One

You and me are a miracle!

We can start exploring the truth by asking the following questions: What is the origin of our Universe? How come our planet Earth has the right conditions for life? How do you and me come to exist? Where did we come from? How did you become you? And how your brain (the hardware) and the mind (the software) influence your body and your behavior? The answer to each one of these questions would reveal as you go through this book, that you and me are a miracle with trillions of events occurring exactly as they should to keep us alive and enjoy this wonderful world we live in.

The first miracle is the Universe itself and the planet Earth which sustains life. The nature of our Universe is remarkably sensitive to just six numbers as suggested by Martin Rees, that describe and define everything from the way atoms are held together to the amount of matter in our Universe. The physical laws that govern the Universe with billions of galaxies, stars and planets depend on these overwhelmingly large and small numbers. Stars, planets and humans would not exist if there is a small change in any one of these numbers. The properties of the quantum world such as type, number, size and mass of atoms and sub-atomic particles and the forces linking them together determine the chemistry of our everyday world and there by our life itself. If any of these values were "un-tuned", there would be no stars and no life as we know it in our current Universe. This understanding offers a radically new perspective on our place in the Universe and on the deep forces that shape, quite simply, everything. If you and me could exist and even have the curiosity to understand the reasons for our existence, it is because of the incredible right combination of these six numbers.

If we imagine that our Big Bang wasn't the only one, then there would be some, which have the essential tuning for life to emerge and we find ourselves in just that Universe. It appears as if the Universe evolved in a way that is exactly right for us, leading to human life on this planet Earth. The reasons why these numbers are exactly the way they are, would be still beyond comprehension – amazing

2

and inspiring to continue the search for reasons and better understanding of the reality.

Earth, our home, is a fascinating planet of all planets in the Solar System, since it is the only planet that supports life according to information available till now. Earth is the densest and the only planet to have large parts of it covered with water. Earth has a strong magnetic field, which protects us from cosmic radiation. Frank Drake estimated the probability of finding advanced civilization such as ours in the Milky Way, which could be millions of them but the average distance between two such planets could be 200 light years! Out of over ten billion trillion planets, scientists have discovered about seventy planets outside the Solar System. So we can't speak with authority on this matter. If you look for a planet suitable for life, you have to be really lucky and the more advanced the life, the luckier you have to be. The factors which made life possible on the planet Earth are its location, its interior, the moon, timing of various events, atmosphere and the presence of water.

The second miracle is the evolution of life from simple microbes to intelligent humans. Life arose rapidly and early in Earth's history – as soon as Earth could possibly support it. How life began is arguably one of the most thought provoking questions of our time but the first forms of life would have been very much simpler than anything that we see around us. They must have had the ability to grow and reproduce which is the fundamental property and be subject to Darwinian evolution. So it might be that the primitive things that actually fit the definition were little strands of nucleic acids. It is generally accepted that before DNA, there was an "RNA world". Single-stranded RNA is more stable and replicates better under certain conditions. Molecules spontaneously self-assembled into droplets that enclose a watery solution and maintain a chemical environment different from their surroundings and they are called protobionts. Thus, protobiont with self-replicating RNA really does represent a primitive form of life, which is considered the first in transitioning from nonliving to living. Several hypotheses describe the assimilation of chemicals into an order that responds to the environment in a living sort of way.

Living things have evolved into three large clusters of closely related organisms called "domains" namely archaea, bacteria and eukaryota. Archaea and bacteria are small, unicellular and relatively simple cells with a circular strand of DNA containing their genes and they are called prokaryotes. Nearly all the life – including plants, animals and we humans – belong to the third domain, eukaryota. Eukaryotic cells are more complicated than prokaryotes – the DNA is linear and found within a nucleus. Evidence supports the idea that eukaryotic cells are actually the descendants of separate prokaryotic cells that joined together in a symbiotic union – a phenomenon known as endosymbiosis. Finally, we humans are vertebrates and are subjected to the same evolutionary principles that govern all life on the planet. Thus, life consists of a ladder leading from lowly microbes to lofty humanity.

The third miracle is the incredible cell which keeps us alive and the transformation of a single cell into a baby. We understand a little of how cells do the things they do - such as growth and development of the body and the brain, maintaining balance by doing things like controlling the flow of blood, protecting the body from pathogens and just keeping us alive. There are about 100 trillion cells in each one of us and each one of them is designed to perform unique and essential life functions. Their role varies depending on their involvement in functions such as respiration, growth, digestion, circulation, communication, movement, reproduction, control and coordination. Cells not only perform routine functions of the human body, but they even know how to overcome the stress by releasing different types of substances into the blood. For example, by nature nitric oxide is a very formidable toxin but scientists found it as an ubiquitous elixir being produced in a curiously devoted manner in human cells aiding in the control of the flow of blood and the energy levels of cells. Nitroglycerine

4

is converted into nitric oxide in the blood stream relaxing the muscle linings of vessels allowing blood to flow more freely.

Human life starts as a single cell – a fertilized egg containing genes, half from the mother and half from the father. Human's personal body plan is written in their genes and to make a new person, the fertilized egg has to divide – making first two, then four, eight and eventually trillions of cells! After just forty seven doublings the embryo has ten thousand trillion cells in their body and is ready to spring forth as a human being. Each of those cells knows exactly what to do – from the moment of conception to its last breath. So, you have no secrets from your cells and they preserve and nurture you and know far more about you than you do.

The transformation of a single cell into a baby remains one of biology's deepest enigmas. Life's most profound mystery – the creation of a new human being – starts with the union of egg and sperm and ends, nine months later, with a baby. How

does an egg, a tiny squishy blob of a cell, grow into a fully formed organism – a perfect human baby? At conception, fertilization is an event that occurs between two haploid cells – an ovum and a sperm cell which combine to form a single diploid cell known as "zygote". Such zygotes contain DNA derived from both parents and this provides all the genetic information necessary to form a new individual. The zygote divides, multiplies and differentiates into millions of cells that form various organ systems and structures of our body. This intricate progression and vast transformation towards fetal development is regulated by the inherited genes.

Many of the most important and least understood stages of a human embryo development take place during the first twenty one days of pregnancy before the mother even knows she's pregnant and while the embryo is still incredibly small, which is less than two millimeters. But even at twenty one days, the embryo is much more than just a simple ball of primitive cells. Its gender, top and bottom, basic body plan, left and right, front and back are already established and developmental future of every cell in the embryo is already set.

It takes two months to form the human embryo – a process known as embryogenesis. After eight weeks of pregnancy, the embryo has all the organs and tissues found in a newborn baby – although many exist in primitive form. During the last seven months of pregnancy, the fetus (no longer called as an embryo) continues to grow, but the fundamental blueprint for the baby is established during embryogenesis. The zygote starts its journey that, over nine months, produces descendant cells with a huge variety of shapes and functions like: bone cells, nerve cells, red and white blood cells, the cells of eyes, fingernails, stomach and skin. It is an astonishing journey and it all starts with a single cell!

The fourth miracle is that you are unique, even though most of the genes are same in all humans. We share some characteristics with our parents and our family members, but still every one of us has a unique combination of traits. There is no one else exactly like you – it's only you! Some traits are controlled by genes that pass from parent to child, some are acquired through learning and most of them are influenced by a combination of genes and environmental factors. We can understand from our genome sequence that our DNA and associated genes define us – our appearance, physiology and behavior. Everything about our body, from eyes to the toes, is the expression of genes which is the culmination of gene regulation and protein synthesis. Thus, genes influence the traits you inherited in predictable and unpredictable ways.

Genetic variations arise mainly through sexual reproduction (meiosis, recombination/crossing over), independent assortment (random pattern of inheritance), gene flow (movement of genes from one population to another) and the very important DNA mutations. Independent assortment during the formation of gametes itself creates 2^{23} combinations which is equivalent to 80 trillion possible variations from the parent. As the environments are unstable, populations that are genetically variant will be able to adapt to changing situations better than those that do not contain genetic variation. Genetic variation permits flexibility and survival of a population in the face of changing environmental circumstances.

The fifth miracle is your body and brain. Every single breath and heartbeat requires a brilliantly designed inner system of devices, engines, circuitry and software. Your body integrates a number of biological systems that carry out specific functions necessary for everyday living. The human body is a marvel of bio-mechanical engineering. The harmony among the interconnected systems is like a symphony producing the works of Mozart or Beethoven with all individual systems and organs working in concert. The average adult takes over 20,000 breaths a day and his/her lungs inhale over two million liters of air every day. Your heart must pump 75 gallons of blood an hour, 2000 gallons every

day or 67,500 gallons in an year. The heart beats around 3 billion times in an average person's life and pumps about 1 million barrels of blood during an average lifetime! The body creates new cells to replace dying cells, to maintain, defend and repair itself. Cells join together to make up tissues (epithelial, connective, muscles and nerves), tissues unite to form organs and organs work together as an organ system. Each one of those organs does amazing things. Your eyes, for example are very sensitive and on a very clear night can find the galaxy of Andromeda which is about 2.5 million light years away – an inconceivable distance indeed!

The human brain is made up of 100 billion nerve cells. Each and every cell is connected to around 10,000 others. If it is so, the total number of connections in your brain is about 100 trillion. Your brain is unique as its connections are the result of everything you learnt and experienced as a child. Your brain started to wire itself up before you were born and carried on until you were two years old.

7

Mind is the activity of the nervous system including brain. The physical brain and nervous system are the mechanisms by which energy and information flow throughout our body. The sensory organs receive information from the environment which is converted into electrical signals that travel through the nervous system and to the brain finally. Then the brain gives them meaning based on its own conditioning and responds by releasing neurotransmitters and sending electrical signals which in turn regulate the body, control movement and influence emotions. Your brain changes throughout your life. Each and every experience you have will impact the structure of your brain. A changing brain enables you to learn, remember and adapt to your surroundings. The brain undergoes a pruning process in teenage years removing connections that are seldom or never used. Even the adult brain is now thought to be far more adaptable than was formerly believed. The steady formation of new neurons in adults may represent more than merely 'patching up' the ageing brain. New neurons may give the adult brain the same learning ability that a young brain is endowed with, still keeping the existing mature circuits intact to maintain stability.

Let us start exploring these five miracles in some detail to understand more about ourselves.

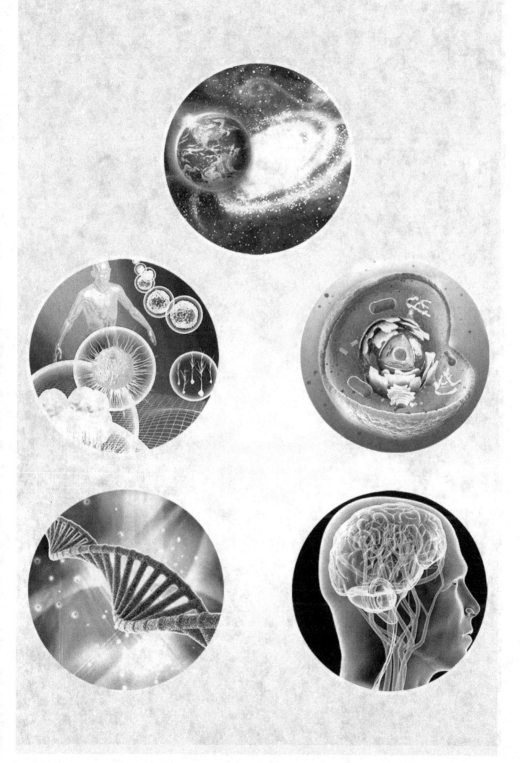

Chapter Two

The first miracle:
The Universe itself and our planet
Earth which sustains life

The defining moment in the creation of our Universe called Big Bang is supposed to have happened about 13.7 billion years ago. Our Universe is at least a hundred billion light years across with a vast array of huge galaxies, stars, planets and almost an infinite number of tiny particles such as photons, protons, electrons, neutrons and many more. This 'visible Universe' – the Universe we know and can talk about is a million, million, million, million miles across or around ten billion light years across with about 100 billion galaxies and each galaxy having about 100 billion stars. According to Martin Rees, 'the meta Universe' – the Universe at large is vastly roomier and a number of light years to the edge of the Universe would be written with millions of zeros!

The planet Earth which is one of the planets around Sun, just one star among billions of stars in Milky Way galaxy, has taken 4.5 billion years for the emergence of human life. The forces and particles at the micro as well as macro level are governed by mathematical laws which influence the way the Universe evolves.

Six amazing numbers!

Martin Rees in his book "Just Six Numbers" says that things would not be as they are even if there is very slight change in the value of these six numbers. He says that these six numbers, which determine the expansion of the Universe and the forces governing it, are basically the recipe for our Universe. These six fundamental numbers are: D – the number of dimensions we live in; N – the ratio of the strength of gravity to that of electromagnetism; Epsilon (ϵ) – the ratio of mass lost to energy when hydrogen is fused to form helium; Omega (Ω) – the density parameter describing the amount of dark matter; Lambda (λ) – representing new 'antigravity' force that controls the expansion of our Universe; and Q – the ratio between the rest mass energy of matter and force of gravity.

Each one of these six numbers plays a crucial and distinctive role in our Universe, and collectively determine how the Universe evolves. These numbers influence the size and form of our Universe and its elements, the space in which it expands and life span itself. The Universe is so sensitive to the value of these six numbers that if there is any minor change in their values, there would be no stars and no life. For example, the balance between the nuclear forces and the astoundingly feeble power of gravity, giving us N, is a huge number involving 36 zeroes and if it is less by few zeros, we wouldn't be here. If the gravity is a little too strong, the Universe would collapse upon itself to a point of singularity and if it is weak the Universe will keep racing away until everything is so far apart that there is no chance for material interactions. There should be a perfect balance which ensures that gravity would be strong enough to cancel any infinite expansion of the Universe and yet weak enough to prevent the premature collapse of the Universe. Everything is just right so far and cosmologists call this the Goldilocks effect. If the gravitational force were larger (N is smaller), the matter would collapse

much faster into smaller spheres, galaxies would form much more quickly and they would be much smaller in size. The stars would be so densely packed precluding stable planetary systems, which are a prerequisite for life. This Universe could have been short-lived and there would be no time for evolution to lead to intelligent life. The Universe would be very much different from the present Universe, and life would not be able to exist. If the gravitation force is much smaller (N is larger) the early Universe would have expanded too fast for the formation of galaxies. It is just a miracle that we evolved and came to exist as we are with just the right combination of these numbers. We should indeed be grateful that our expanding Universe is just right for us.

Fine-tuned Universe

J.B.S. Haldane once famously observed "The Universe is not only queerer than we suppose; it is queerer than we can suppose". Martin Rees believes that there are many Universes, possibly an infinite number, each with different attributes in different combinations and that we simply live in one that combines things in the way that allows us to exist. He further says that our Universe could not exist but for the special requisite tuning in the fundamental numbers that govern it. He also observes that there were many Big Bangs it shouldn't come as any surprise that in some of them the tuning is fulfilled for life to emerge and we find ourselves in just that Universe. It is difficult to comprehend why these numbers are exactly the way they are and we continue the search for reasons and better understanding of the reality. You and me could exist and even have the curiosity to understand the reasons for our existence as the Universe is tuned to these just right values with extraordinary coherence and precision.

Milky Way Galaxy

Milky Way is just one of the more than 100 billion galaxies in the visible Universe and estimates suggest that there could be more than 100 billion stars in the Milky Way and the Sun

is just one of those stars. Our Solar System may be the liveliest thing for trillions of miles but all the visible stuff in it including the Sun, planets and their moons, billions of asteroids, comets and others fill just one trillionth of the available space. According to Carl Sagan the probable planets in the Universe at large could be 10 billion trillion and the amount of space through which they are lightly scattered would be beyond imagination. He wrote "If we are randomly inserted into the Universe, the chances we would be on or near a planet would be less than one in a billion trillion trillion".

Sun and its Family

Sun is one of a few hundred billion stars in the Milky Way galaxy, which together form a flattened disc shaped system which is roughly a hundred thousand light years across and a couple of thousand light years thick. The Sun is a very important star from our perspective as our own evolution is tied closely to the evolution of the Solar System. It is a huge star which consists of around 98% material in the Solar System. Our Sun is formed about five billion years ago, completing about twenty orbits from its life time to date and is half way through its life cycle as of now. The cloud of stuff from which Sun and its family formed consists of mostly hydrogen and helium. The protons of four hydrogen nuclei combine to make one helium nucleus. The total mass of the helium nucleus (alpha particle) is 0.7 percent less than the mass of four protons and this difference in the mass is converted into pure energy every time the synthesis of hydrogen atoms into helium happens. Five million tons of mass has been converted into pure energy every second in the last five billion years! The mass equivalent of energy radiated so far is about hundred times the mass of the Earth. The Sun would consume all the hydrogen present in it and may become 'white dwarf' after another five to six billion years or so. Until then, we need not worry about our source of energy.

Although many people refer to the Sun as a big ball of fire, the Sun can more accurately be described as a thermonuclear reactor composed of hot plasma and strong magnetic fields. The Sun itself is composed of mostly hydrogen and helium, with a small percent being made up of 48 other elements like oxygen, carbon, neon and iron. The Sun, due to its huge size and temperature variations, exhibits differential rotation; it rotates once in every 23.5 days. The Sun's core produces gamma rays that travel from the core to outer surface and by the time it reaches the surface, it is primarily visible light. Sun also emits a low density stream of charged particles (mostly electrons and protons) known as the solar wind which propagates throughout the Solar System at about 450 km/sec. The solar wind and the highly charged particles ejected by solar flares can have dramatic effects on the Earth ranging from power line surges to radio interference to the beautiful aurora borealis (the "Northern Lights" caused by the interaction between the charged particles from the Sun, Earth's magnetic field and atmospheric molecules).

The Solar System has planets that orbit our Sun and their respective moons, in addition to the comets, asteroids, dwarf planets, dust and gas. Eight planets form the most obvious members of the Sun's family – after excluding Pluto which is recently dropped from the list of planets in Solar System by the International committee on astronomy. The Solar System is about two-thirds of the way out from the center to the edge of the disc (Milky Way galaxy) orbiting around the center of the disc. It takes about 225 million years to complete one orbit, at a speed of 250 km per second and this time period is called cosmic year. The stars of the disc form in groups out of a single large, collapsing cloud of gas and dust. The Sun has a Magnetosphere (Heliosphere/ Magnetic Field) extending beyond Pluto. The planets near the Sun such as Mercury and Venus probably had some liquid in their early days, but were completely burnt out due to their proximity to Sun. Scientists say that if Earth had been even slightly closer, there wouldn't have had any life due to the Sun's extreme heat.

The planets

Mercury

Mercury is the closest planet to the Sun, named after the Roman messenger God. Mercury is fast and takes only 88 days to revolve around the Sun. The diameter around the equator is 4879 km. It is the second densest planet in the Solar System after the Earth. The only spacecraft to approach Mercury so far has been NASA's Mariner. It has observed various aspects of the atmosphere and surface of Mercury. Mercury has thin atmosphere consisting of oxygen, helium and hydrogen. The magnetic field exerted by Mercury is only 1% of Earth's magnetic field. The main elements found on Mercury are sodium, potassium and iron and the surface conditions are harshest. Daytime temperature rises to about 425°C, hot enough to melt lead and hotter than any planet except Venus. Because of lack of substantial atmosphere to retain heat, in the night time the temperature drops quickly to around −180°C which is among the coldest found in the Solar System. This range of −180°C at night to 425°C in the day is the second largest surface temperature variation in the Solar System. Because of it's horrific temperature extremes mercury is not suitable for life.

Venus

Venus is also known as evening star. It is the brightest planet to appear to the naked eye. The name Venus was given to it from the ancient Goddess of Beauty. There have been many expeditions that have attempted to study the atmosphere and surface of Venus. The first one was Mariner 2 in the year 1962. Venus has 82 percent of the mass of Earth and a diameter of about 12,104 km. The atmosphere consists of 98 percent carbon and 2 percent nitrogen with traces of few other gases. There is a great temperature variation on Venus varying from 462°C to −170°C and hence not suitable for life.

Mars

Mars is the last terrestrial planet in the Solar System and the name is given from the ancient God of War.

It is a reddish planet with swathes of orange. Scientists say that Mars is red as the surface is highly oxidized iron. They for many years have believed that there could be life on Mars, as they opined that there is ice and methane on Mars. Future expeditions will find out more about this aspect.

Jupiter

Jupiter is the biggest planet of Solar System. Its name is the Roman equivalent of Greek God Zeus who was the father of all Gods. Jupiter with a diameter of 143,000 km and mass 318 times the mass of the Earth is the largest planet in the Solar System. It's magnetic field is 14 times as powerful as Earth. Jupiter is famous for the big red spot on its surface. The planet is a gas giant composed mainly of hydrogen and helium. There is virtually no water to support life. On this planet there is no solid surface for life to develop anywhere except as a floating microscopic organism. Hence, it is also not suitable for life.

Saturn

Saturn is the sixth planet of the Solar System. Saturn is a smaller Jupiter with diameter 9.4 times that of Earth and a mass 95 times that of Earth. It has a beautiful appearance with the famous rings which are mostly made of rocks and ice. The atmosphere of rings has mostly molecular hydrogen and oxygen. From the Earth, though they look continuous, the rings are composed of innumerable small particles, each of them moving in an independent orbit. These rings range in size from a centimeter or so to several meters. The voyager Cassini revealed more about the rings and other features such as the spokes of the rings. Satellites around Saturn include Titan which has a thick atmosphere made of nitrogen and methane. Titan may provide a chance for life in the Solar System while Europa the moon of Jupiter is also considered to have possibility for life (far in the future when Sun nears the end of life). The planet is comprised almost entirely of hydrogen and helium and trace amounts of water ice in its lower cloud deck. Cloud temperatures dip down to -150°C, hence not suitable for life.

Uranus

The name is derived from the Greek God of Sky. It was discovered by Sir William Herschel, but believed that it was a comet. Uranus was thus the first planet to be discovered, as it was not visible to the ancients. It has no solid surface and is mostly composed of ices: water, ammonia and methane and then it is covered by an atmosphere of hydrogen and helium. Uranus is really cold. Its cloud tops measure -224°C, and then it gets warmer inside down to the core, which has a temperature of 4726°C. Hence Uranus is unable to support the kinds of living organisms that exist on Earth.

Neptune

Neptune is known for its great winds that are the fastest for any planet in the Solar System. The winds blow at a speed of 2500 Km/h, hence Neptune is considered as a gas giant. The planet is just made of gases with no solid material. It remains unlikely that a planet with such a volatile and chemically disparate atmosphere could harbor life.

Earth

The planet Earth, which supports life with intelligence such as humans, is very precious. Earth our home is a fascinating planet, since it is the only planet in the Solar System that supports life according to information available till now. It is the densest planet in the Solar System and the only planet to have large parts of it covered with water. Earth is subjected to a lot of volcanic and seismic activities like continental drift, tectonic plates, tsunamis and periodic global warming and cooling. Earth has a strong magnetic field due to its iron core and tilt in its axis. Earth moves from west to east at 20 km/sec and this causes the various drifts and continental shifts. Factors which made life possible on the planet Earth are:

Earth's location

It is a sort of miracle that the planet Earth is located at the right distance from Sun which is big enough to receive good amount of energy, but not so big enough to burn itself out. It is also well chosen and suited for us to orbit where we do. If the distance is too much closer everything on Earth would have evaporated and if it is farther away, everything would have frozen. Earth would have been uninhabitable had it been just 1 percent farther from or 5 percent closer to the Sun.

Earth's interior

The interior of the Earth is like a layered onion, with three main shells namely Crust, Mantle and Core. Each layer is further divided in to two parts: Oceanic crust and Continental crust; Upper mantle and Lower mantle; Upper core and Lower core. The crust is extended up to 30 km in depth inside the inner surface of the Earth. The Upper mantle is extended up to 720 km inside the interior of the Earth. The Lower mantle has a thickness of about 2171 km. The types of rocks that are found in Lower mantle are magnesium rocks and silicon oxides. The Outer core has a thickness of 2259 km. The types of rocks or minerals found in the Outer core are iron, oxygen, sulfur and nickel alloy. The Inner core has a thickness of 1221 km. Although the core and mantle are almost of equal thickness, the actual core forms only 15% of the Earth's volume, whereas the mantle occupies 84%. The crust makes up the remaining 1%. The total thickness of Earth's inner surface is 6401 km. Our planet is having a molten interior with magma swirling around beneath us. The atmosphere which shields us from cosmic radiation is a result of the outgassing due to the molten interior.

Earth's magnetic field

Earth's core is definitely the hottest part of our planet. It is made up of metals entirely. The outer core is mostly made of iron and nickel. They form an alloy which is very hot at temperature 4000 to 5000°C. Although the temperatures are extremely high, the pressure due to gravity in the inner core will be too high which makes the iron to remain solid even in such harsh temperatures. The inner core of the Earth spins on its axis. The outer core also spins along with the inner core, but at a different rate, which leads to a creation of the dynamo effect. The flow of liquid iron in the outer core is responsible for the generation of conventional current, which in turn causes Earth's magnetic field. Hence Earth acts as a natural giant electromagnet. Since the liquid in the outer core is responsible for the magnetic field of the Earth, it could change the location of the magnetic poles of the Earth as per the rotation of the outer core. The poles actually change places periodically – about 400 times in the last 330 million years. As the charged metals like iron and nickel pass through these magnetic fields, electric currents are generated. This cycle of electric and magnetic fields would be continuous resulting in strong magnetic field of Earth. This process (responsible for the sustained magnetic field) is known as Geodynamo. The planet is magnetic due to metals present in the middle of the Earth's core and the liquid outer core controls the magnetic field of the Earth. This magnetic field acts as a guard to protect the Earth from charged bodies floating in the Solar System. When the solar wind reaches the Earth, the charged particles collide with the magnetosphere, rather than with the atmospheric molecules.

Twin planet

We are a twin planet as our Moon is comparable in size unlike most of the other moons that are tiny in relation to their master planet. We now believe that about 4.5 billion years ago a Mars sized object slammed into Earth, and created the Moon from the debris. This made a big difference to us as our Moon is having steadying influence without which the Earth would wobble like a dying top, with unpredictable consequences for climate and weather. The steady gravitational influence of the Moon keeps the Earth spinning at the right speed and angle to provide the sort of stability necessary for the long and successful development of life.

Atmosphere

We are indeed grateful for having the atmosphere, as it keeps us warm

and alive! Without it, Earth would be a lifeless ball of ice with an average temperature of -51°C. In addition, the atmosphere absorbs or deflects incoming swarms of cosmic rays, charged particles, ultraviolet rays and the like. Altogether the gaseous paddling of the atmosphere is equivalent to a fifteen foot thickness of protective concrete and without it these invisible visitors from space would slice through us like tiny daggers. Even rainfall would pound us senseless if it were not for the atmosphere's slowing drag.

Water

Initially Earth was very hot and volcanic. At first the crust was formed as the planet got cooled. The impacts from asteroids and debris were the reason to form lots of craters. As the time went on, the planet continued to cool, forming water on the surface and this lead to the formation of oceans. The Earth's surface that we have today is a result of lot of eruptions from volcanoes, earthquakes, and several other factors. With its huge diameter and mass, Earth is able to provide gravity that could hold all objects. The surface of the Earth provides a place for the human beings, animals, plants to live as the life evolved from bacteria and virus 4 billion years ago. Later on people came to existence to question why and how it all happened.

The life depends upon water and about two thirds of our planet is covered with water. It is a good solvent that can dissolve a wide range of substances, an efficient thermal conductor and has remarkable surface tension. Water expands on freezing into ice, and the ice floats on surface of the water. If ice sank when it froze, the way solids ought to when freezing out from, then ice would not float on the surface but rather settle at the bottom of lakes and oceans which eventually would freeze everything. There would be no marine life. We are lucky that ice floats, and forms a protective cover.

The angle between two hydrogen atoms in a water molecule is just right for the molecules to form a very open array, in which each oxygen atom is joined not only to its two

regular hydrogen companions in a molecule, but by hydrogen bonds to two other water molecules. Each hydrogen atom is joined in this way to one another oxygen molecule, as well as to its regular molecular partner. The structure that results is similar to the crystalline structure of diamond, though not as strong. It is an open structure, with plenty of space between atoms, and the regular pattern of the lattice array is responsible for example, for the beautiful, regular geometry of the pattern of a snowflake. But the structure is so open that any particular amount of frozen water actually occupies a slightly larger volume than the same amount of liquid water. So it is less dense than water, and floats on water. From his various studies of water and other substances, Henderson concluded "The biologist may now rightly regard the Universe in its very essence as biocentric."

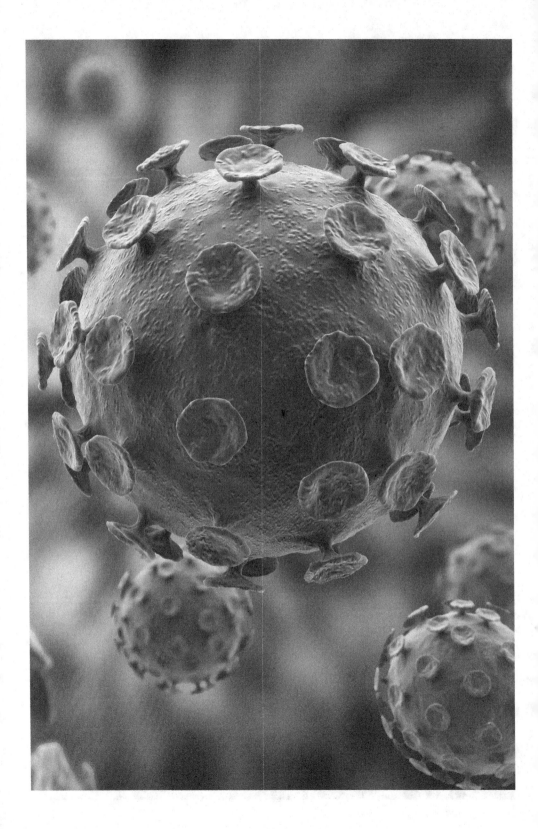

Chapter Three

The second miracle:
Evolution of life from
microbes to humans

How do you and me come to exist?

The Earth is estimated to have been formed about 4.6 billion years ago and Earth's crust was expected to be in molten state for about 600-800 million years before it got solidified. The constituents of Earth's early atmosphere could have been simple molecules like water vapor, carbon dioxide, carbon monoxide, methane, ammonia, nitrogen, hydrogen sulfide and hydrogen. The elements required to create life are contained in these molecules and the energy required for life to evolve primarily comes from the Sun in the form of light.

The Haldane-Oparin hypothesis suggests that life molecules were initially formed from inorganic sources which underwent polymerization to form macro molecules including primitive versions of proteins and enzymes. Oparin believed that life developed from coacervates, tiny microscopic spontaneously formed spherical aggregates of lipid molecules that are held together by electrostatic forces. Coacervates are tiny droplets with a cluster of macro molecules surrounded by membrane-like shell of water molecules. They exhibited the properties of life as they grow and divide. They also developed complex mechanisms to regulate growth and division which eventually produced the first simple cellular life. However it is still not clearly understood whether nucleic acids such as RNA, DNA or enzymes came first as they depend on each other in self-replication. Nucleic acids are required to synthesize polypeptides to form enzymes while enzymes are required to synthesize nucleic acids. It is possible that they originated together as nucleic acids may be considered as a specific form of enzymes and some may exhibit enzyme like character.

The evolution of life started 3.6 billion years ago with simple single-celled organisms called microbes followed by cyanobacteria performing photosynthesis around 200 million years later. Multi-cellular complex organisms exist for nearly one billion years while marine life such as fish evolved around 500

26

million years ago followed by land based plants, insects and creatures. Dinosaurs survived for nearly 135 million years from the beginning of the Jurassic period (about 200 million years ago) until the end of the Cretaceous period (66 million years ago). The end of the Cretaceous however saw the mass extinction of the dinosaurs while some of the mammals survived and expanded after this disaster. Humans first began to evolve nearly 200,000 years ago but the rate of evolution of our species has accelerated since the end of the last ice age which is roughly 10,000 years ago. So the modern human life is very recent in the life of Earth.

The rise of oxygen

The atmosphere on early Earth was strikingly different from that of today. Primeval Earth's atmosphere consisted of hydrogen, methane, ammonia, water vapor and only a negligible amount of free oxygen. This is a very significant aspect because with a lot of free oxygen, life perhaps could not have arisen from inorganic compounds. This is because oxygen aims to oxidize substances, which implies that electrons are removed. Significantly, the early atmosphere was actually highly reductive (capable of gaining electrons and forming more complex molecules).

In one proposed scenario referred to as chemical evolution, the first and foremost organisms arose from a four-stage process. The first stage probably involved the abiotic (not of biological origin) synthesis of small organic molecules (monomers) such as amino acids and nucleotides. Ultraviolet light from the Sun would simply have reached the surface of the Earth (ozone did not exist at that time) and would probably have been the primary source of energy to drive these reactions. In the second stage, these monomers likely joined to form polymers. Two key polymers for any kind of genesis of life would have been proteins and nucleic acids. In the third stage, polymers would have aggregated into protobionts (systems that are considered to have possibly been the precursors to prokaryotic cells), which would have been

Let's look at how humans evolved....

Timeline	Event
4.6 billion years	Circling the Sun, the Earth has harbored an increasing diversity of life forms
3.6 billion years ago	Origin of simple cells (Prokaryotes)
3.4 billion years ago	Origin of cyanobacteria performing photosynthesis
2 billion years ago	Origin of complex cells (Eukaryotes)
1.2 -1 billion years ago	Origin of eukaryotes which sexually reproduce, multicellular life
600 - 400 million years ago	Origin of simple animals, land plants, insects and seeds
360 - 60 million years ago	Origin of amphibians, reptiles, mammals, birds, flowers, primates
20 million years ago	Origin of the family Hominidae (great apes)
250,000 years ago	Origin of the genus Homo (including humans and their predecessors)
200,000 years ago	Origin of anatomically modern humans

separate entities discernible from their surroundings. Finally, these protobionts would have developed some type of heredity mechanism, hence the need for nucleic acids. The microbes or bacterial organisms which remained the only form of life for nearly two billion years produced their heirs by cleaving themselves.

At some point in the first billion years of life, cyanobacteria commonly known as blue green algae learned to tap into a freely available resource – the hydrogen that exists in spectacular abundance in water. They absorbed hydrogen from water molecules and released oxygen which is a kind of photosynthesis.

As Margulis and Sagan note – "Photosynthesis is undoubtedly the most important single metabolic innovation in the history of life on the planet and it was not by plants but by bacteria".

Cyanobacteria trapped micro particle of sand and dust and formed solid structures called stromatolites. Stromatolites are formed, wherever seas were shallow, in different shapes and sizes. They appeared in the form of large size cauliflowers and sometimes as column-like structures. It was an ecosystem by it self as variety of primitive organism lived together.

In 1961 scientists discovered a community of living stromatolites, living remnants of Earth as it was 3.5 billion years ago at Shark Bay on the remote northwest coast of Australia. As Richard Fortey has put it – "This is truly time travelling and if the world were attuned to its real wonders this sight would be as well known as the pyramids of Giza". Release of oxygen in small quantities over last two billion years raised the level of oxygen in Earth's atmosphere to 20 percent and the environment is ready for the next stage of evolution of life.

Prokaryotic evolution

The prokaryotes are a class of organisms that lack a cell nucleus or any other membrane-bound organelles. Bacteria are the major group in prokaryotes and their advancements led to more complex living organisms. It has been considered that the diverse nature of bacteria and archaebacteria resulted from this evolution gradually. Fossil records suggest that mounds of bacteria once covered young Earth. Some began making their own food for them using carbon dioxide in the atmosphere and energy they harvested from the Sun. This process known as photosynthesis produced enough oxygen to change atmosphere on the Earth. Soon afterward, new oxygen-breathing life forms came into existence. With a population of increasingly diverse bacterial life forms, the stage was set for some amazing things to happen. As bacteria modified structures to expand their territory and tolerance, they changed into newer species with diverse structures and functions. Due to their uniqueness in structure and function, bacteria are classified in their own kingdom. Advancements in the morphology and physiology of prokaryotes continued to the juncture where two separate types are now identifiable: bacteria and archaea.

Eukaryotic evolution

It took quite a long time for life to grow complex as the world had to wait until the simpler organisms had oxygenated the atmosphere sufficiently. It took about two billion years for oxygen levels to reach more or less modern levels of optimum concentration in the atmosphere. This was followed by arrival of new type of cells with nucleus and other bodies called organells, known as eukaryotes. This phenomenon is thought to have started when some blundering or adventuresome bacterium either invaded or captured some other bacterium and it turned out that it suited them both equally. The captive bacterium thus became a mitochondrion. This

particular mitochondrial invasion or endosymbiotic event made complex life possible. Similarly, plants invasion produced another organelle called chloroplasts that enabled plants to photosynthesize.

Eukaryotic cells differ in many respects from the generally smaller cells of bacteria and archaea. Even the smallest single-celled eukaryote is far more complex in structure than any prokaryote. Among the most fundamental questions in biology is how these complex eukaryotic cells evolved from much simpler prokaryotic cells. A process called endosymbiosis probably led to mitochondria and plastids (choloroplasts). The theory of endosymbiosis proposes that mitochondria and plastids were formerly small prokaryotes living within larger cells. The word endosymbiont refers to a cell that lives within another cell, which is called host cell.

After the first eukaryotes appeared, a multitude range of unicellular forms evolved, gradually giving rise to the diversity of single-celled eukaryotes that continue to flourish today. But multicellular forms also evolved. Their descendants include a variety of algae, plants, fungi, and animals. Thus, Eukaryotes were bigger – eventually as much as ten thousand times bigger than their simpler cousins and carried as much as a thousand times more DNA. Gradually a system evolved in which life was dominated by two types of organisms – those that expel oxygen like plants, and those that take oxygen in like you and me. Thanks to this innovation big, complicated, visible entities like us were possible. Planet Earth was ready to move on to its next ambitious phase and by about 200,000 years ago, we the Homo sapiens arrived on this planet Earth.

Mass extinctions

Time periods in Earth's life history during which exceptionally large numbers of species go extinct are called mass extinctions. More than 90 percent of all organisms that have ever lived on Earth are almost extinct. As new species evolve to fit ever changing ecological niches,

older species fade into oblivion. But the rate of extinction is far from being constant. At least a handful of times in the last 500 million years, a large number of species on Earth have vanished in a geologic blink of the eye.

Even though these mass extinctions are fatal events, they open up the planet for new life-forms to evolve. Dinosaurs appeared after one of the biggest mass extinction events on planet – the Permian-Triassic extinction about 250 million years ago. The most studied mass extinction about 64 million years ago (Cretaceous and Paleogene periods), wiped away the dinosaurs and made room for mammals to quickly diversify and evolve. The reasons of these mass extinction events are puzzled mysteries, though volcanic eruptions and large asteroids and comets collision with the Earth are prime suspects in many of the cases. These would emit tons of toxic debris into the atmosphere, blacken the skies with smoke etc., for at least several months. Most of the plants and plant-eating creatures would quickly die due to starvation.

Whatever the cause dinosaurs, as well as about half of all species inhabiting the planet, went extinct.

Human Evolution

In our tour of Earth's biodiversity, we come at last to our own species, Homo sapiens. We all humans are vertebrates, and are subjected to evolutionary principles that govern all the life on the planet Earth. However, we are a relatively new species though our hominid (also called ape) ancestors might date back to 20 million years in the past. Modern humans (those who learned agriculture and demonstrated tool use and complex social structure) dates back to just 100,000 years ago. A number of characters distinguish humans from other hominoids. Most obviously, humans stand upright and walk on two legs. Humans have a much larger brain than other hominoids and are capable of using language, symbolic thought, manufacture and the use of complex tools. Humans also have reduced jaw bones and muscles, along with a shorter digestive tract. The list of derived human characters at the molecular level is growing as

scientists compare the genomes of humans and chimpanzees. Although the two genomes are 99% identical, a disparity of 1% can translate into a large number of differences in a genome that contains 3 billion base pairs.

Thus, the evolution of our species from an ape-like ancestor has been a very convoluted process. Some human traits like bipedalism evolved very early during the evolution. Yet other traits like large brains evolved very recently. A look at our lineage would show many side branches and evolutionary dead ends with some of the species that prevailed for million years simply fading away into oblivion. The robust australopiths (a fossil bipedal primate with both ape-like and human characteristics) is an example of one such species. Whatever their origins, these evolutionary accidents took us on a 6-million-year journey from something similar to a great ape to us, Homo sapiens. Our evolution is a result of genetic luck, environmental changes and geological chance. One wonders where the next six million years might take us!

Mechanisms that drive evolution

Evolution is the process by which modern organisms have descended from ancient ancestors. This is responsible for both the remarkable similarities we see across all life forms and the amazing diversity they display. It is a puzzle as to how organisms survive and adapt in various environments post their evolution. How exactly does evolution work? There are different phenomena that generated a change in the evolution mechanism which made the organisms survive and adapt to the varied environments and they are as follows:

Adaptation

Adaptation is the condition of organisms being well designed for life in their environments. It refers to all the behavioral, functional and structural characteristics and aspects that enhance the organism's survival and reproductive success in its natural environment and circumstances. Thus, the webbed feet of ducks or otters are adaptations to living in water, enabling them to swim more efficiently than before. In physiology, adaptation is said to occur in sense organs when the sensitivity of an organ alters in response to changes in environmental conditions. The beak of the woodpecker and the Galapagos finches are examples of such phenomenon. The beak of woodpecker elongated as a natural phenomenon to adapt to its requirement of pecking the wood. The variation in shape and size of beaks in Galapagos finches is because of the variety in food that is available in their environment. All evolutionary changes are the result of adaptation and can be explained by natural selection.

Gene flow

It is an evolutionary mechanism that occurs during the migration of individuals from one group to another. When the migrating individuals interbreed with the local population, gene flow in the population is established. Gene flow tends to increase the similarity between remaining populations of the same species because it makes gene pools more similar to one another.

Genetic drift

Genetic drift occurs when a small group of individuals leaves a population and establishes a new one in a geographically isolated area. For example, when a small population of fish is placed in a lake or pond, the fish population will evolve into one that is different from the original.

Natural selection

Darwin wrote in summarizing his concept of the Origin of Species by Means of Natural Selection – "Thus, from the war of nature, from famine and death, the most exalted object of which we are capable of conceiving, namely, the production of the higher animals, directly follows". The most important influence on evolution is natural selection that occurs when an organism is subject to its environment. The fittest organisms survive and contribute their genes to their offspring, generating a population that is better adapted to the environment. The genes of less-fit organisms are eventually lost. Environmental fitness may be expressed in several ways. Some of the examples are: it may involve an individual's ability to avoid and hide from predators, it may imply a greater resistance to disease, it may be the enhanced ability to obtain food and requirements, or it may mean resistance to drought conditions. Fitness may also be measured as enhanced reproductive capability, such as in the ability to attract or initiate a mating process. Better adapted individuals produce relatively more offspring and pass on their genes more efficiently than less adapted individuals.

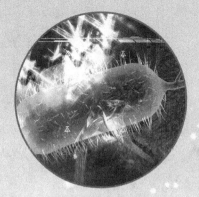

Simple cells
prokaryotes

Cyanobacteria

Eukaryotes (Fungi)

Plants and animals

Primates

Modern humans

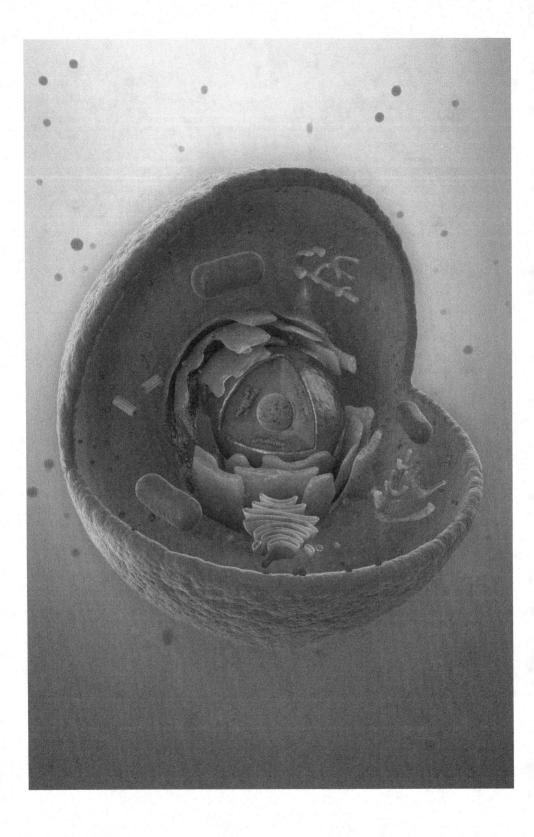

Chapter Four

The third miracle:
The incredible cell which
keeps you alive

Cell – the basic unit of life

The human body contains nearly 100 trillion cells and all of them are working in harmony with each other. Your body is made up of about 200 different types of cells, all of them working together, day and night and each one of them must make the molecules it needs to survive, grow, multiply and do its job. At the center of the cell is the nucleus, which contains a copy of your genes, the instructions for making proteins. Each cell carries a copy of the complete genetic code – the "instruction manual" for your body. So it knows not only how to perform its job but every other job in the body. For example, we do not have to remind a cell to keep an eye on its ATP levels.

Every cell in nature is a thing of wonder and even the simplest are far beyond the limits of human ingenuity. Your cells are a country of ten thousand trillion citizens, each dedicated in some intensively specific way to your overall well-being. There is not a thing they do not do for you. They let you feel pleasure and form thoughts. They extract the nutrients, distribute the energy and carry off the wastes. They also remember to make you hungry in the first place and reward you with a feeling of well-being afterward so that you won't forget to eat again. They will jump to your defense the moment you are threatened and they will unhesitatingly die for you – billions of them daily. So let us take a moment now to regard them with the wonder and appreciation they deserve and thank each one of them.

The cells in the bodies of all but the simplest multicellular animals, both aquatic and terrestrial, exist in an "internal sea" of extracellular fluid enclosed within the integument animal. The cells get nutrients from this fluid. The basic knowledge of cell biology is essential to an understanding of the organ systems in the body. The specialization of the cells in the different organs is considerable, and no cell can be called "typical" of all cells in the body. However, a number of structures (organelles) are common to most cells.

The cells vary enormously in size and shape: the nerve cells, whose filaments can stretch to many feet, to minute disc shaped RBCs, to the rod shaped photocells that provide us the vision. On an average, however a human cell is about twenty microns wide – that is about two hundredths of a millimeter which is too small to be seen but roomy enough to hold thousands of complicated structures like mitochondria and millions upon millions of molecules. The occupants in that tiny cell, especially the lively proteins (about 100 million in each cell) would be spinning, pulsating and flying into each other up to a billion times a second. Enzymes are themselves a type of proteins, performing up to a thousand tasks a second; busily building and rebuilding molecules with inconceivable frenzy. As de Duve notes "The molecular world must necessarily remain entirely beyond the powers of our imagination owing to the incredible speed with which things happen in it".

Nerve cells

Nerve cells, also called as neurons, form part of the nervous system process and transfer information. They are the core components of the spinal cord, brain and peripheral nerves. They use chemical synapses that can induce electrical signals, called action potentials for transmission of signals throughout the body. Nerve cells are good at initiating and conducting electrical signals, often over long distances. A signal may initiate new electrical signals in other nerve cells, or it may stimulate a gland cell to secrete substances or a muscle cell to contract. Thus, nerve cells facilitate a major means of controlling the activities of other cells. The incredible complexity of connections between nerve cells underlies such phenomena as consciousness, perception and learning. These are the final results of the incredible complexity of connections and actions between nerve cells.

Epithelial, Exocrine and Endocrine cells

Epithelial cells are functional for the selective secretion and absorption of ions and organic molecules, and for protection. They are present mainly at the surfaces that cover the body or individual organs, and they also line the walls of various tubular and hollow structures within the body. The epithelial cells at the surface of the skin form a barrier that prevents most of the substances in the external environment to enter directly through the skin.

Exocrine cells secrete products through ducts, such as sweat, mucus or digestive enzymes. The products of these cells reach directly to the target organ. For example, the bile juice from the gall bladder is carried directly into the duodenum via the bile duct.

Endocrine cells are similar to exocrine cells, but they secrete their products directly into the bloodstream instead of through a duct. These cells are present throughout the body but are concentrated more in hormone secreting glands such as pituitary gland. The products of the endocrine cells go throughout the body in the blood stream but act on specific organs by receptors on the cells of the targeted organs.

Connective tissue (CT) cells

CT cells connect, anchor, and support the structures of the body. Some of the CT cells are found in the loose meshwork of cells and fibers underlying most epithelial layers. The complete framework of the skeleton and the different specialized connective tissues, from the crown of the head to the toes, determine the form of the body and act as an entity. The cells responsible for the production of connective tissue are known as fibroblasts. The interconnections between the fibers, the extracellular matrix and the water, together, form the pliable connective tissue as a whole. CT cells make up a variety of physical structures including tendons and the connective framework of fibers in capsules, muscles and ligaments around joints, cartilage, adipose tissues, and lymphatic tissues.

Blood Cells

Red blood cells (RBC or erythrocytes) and white blood cells (WBC or leukocytes) are two types of blood cells. RBC collect oxygen in the lungs and deliver it through the blood to the body tissues. Gaseous exchange is carried out by simple diffusion. WBC are produced in the bone marrow and help the body to fight infectious disease and foreign objects in the immune system. They are found in the lymphatic system, circulatory system, spleen, and other body tissues.

Cells for growth and development

The growth hormones secreted by the master of all the endocrine glands – pituitary gland influence the height and size of the human body. The growth process takes place in two different ways. Some cells increase their volume and some cells divide and multiply. Growth hormones act on all the body's cells. Each and every cell understands the meaning of the message reaching it from the pituitary gland. During the development stage, the growth hormone acts on each individual cell. Each cell develops to the extent commanded by the growth hormone. Thus the individual grows and turns into adult. The pituitary gland directs all the cells in the body and enables them to grow by either increasing their volume or dividing and multiplying. This immaculate phenomenon once again proves the knowledge and precision in the creation of every point in the human body, as trillions of chemical and physical events take place in the depths of the human body outside the individual's knowledge and will.

Proteins are the "workhorse" molecules of life, taking part in every structure and activity of life. Amino acids are the basic structural building units of proteins. Whenever the cell needs to make a specific protein, specialized machinery within the cell's nucleus reads the gene and then uses that information to produce a molecular message in the form of RNA, a molecule very similar to DNA molecule. RNA then moves from the nucleus to the cytoplasm of the cell, where the cell's protein making machinery, the "ribosome" reads the message and produces a protein that exactly matches the specifications in the gene. The protein further travels to the part of the cell where it is needed and begins to work. Some proteins speed up chemical reactions, while others play an important role in structural support, storage, transport, cellular communications and defense against foreign substances. Proteins play a profound role in proper cell function, thus affecting the whole organism.

Enzymes are absolutely necessary to sustain life and they work together co-operating with vitamins and minerals. They act as a catalyst to accelerate chemical reactions because most of the chemical reactions in biological cells would occur too slowly. In enzymatic reactions, the molecules at the beginning of the process known as substrates are converted into different molecules known as products. Almost all chemical reactions in a biological cell need enzymes in order to occur at rates sufficient for life. They work within the cells to regulate

detoxification and produce energy. Enzymes carry out most of the reactions involved in metabolism and catabolism, as well as in RNA synthesis, DNA replication and DNA repair. When the body has an abundance of enzymes, it can easily protect itself and repair the damage from almost all degenerative disease and disorders. Without enzymes, we get diseases earlier in life; we age more quickly and acquire physical impairments and mental retardation as our bodies degenerate.

Cell multiplication and division

The cell cycle is made up of stages in which the cell grows and rests, copies its entire DNA, and divides into two new cells. The cells multiply and grow through a process called mitosis. Before a cell can divide, it must unravel its chromosomes and copy its entire DNA, so that each new cell will get a complete copy. After copying its DNA, a cell normally divides into two new cells. Each new cell gets a complete copy of the entire DNA, bundled up as 46 chromosomes. Cells reproduce themselves by dividing. A "mother" cell divides into two "daughter" cells that are exactly like the mother cell. After growing for a while, these two cells divide eventually to make four cells. Most human cells are "diploid", which means that they have two complete sets of 23 chromosomes and when it divides, each daughter cell also receives two complete sets of chromosomes. Thus, through mitosis, each daughter cell can keep on dividing – from one cell all the way to a trillion.

Meiosis is a specialized process by which germ cells divide to produce gametes. Because the chromosome number of a species remains the same from one generation to the next one, the chromosome number of germ cells must be reduced by half during meiosis. To achieve this, meiosis, unlike mitosis, requires a single round of DNA replication followed by two rounds of cell division. Recombination is one of the most distinguishing factors in meiosis when compared with mitosis, in which chromosomes exchange segments with one another. As a result, the gametes produced during meiosis are genetically unique which creates genetic diversity with each one of them containing 23 chromosomes. The outcome of meiosis is four haploid cells (genetically unique) unlike two diploid cells (genetically identical) produced from mitosis. Thus meiotic processes produce recombinational genetic variation.

Transformation of a single cell into a baby

Life started when a sperm from your father fertilized one of your mother's eggs. About nine months later you were born: a mass of billions of cells! When a sperm cell enters the mother's egg cell, the resulting cell is known as zygote. The zygote contains all of the genetic information needed to produce a multi-cellular organism. It spends the next few days traveling down the Fallopian tube and divides to form a ball of cells. The zygote continues to divide gradually forming an inner most group of cells with an outer shell. This particular stage is called a blastocyst stage. The inner group of cells will transform into the embryo, while the outer group of cells will become the membranes that nourish and protect it. The blastocyst reaches the womb uterus around fifth day and implants into the uterine wall on about day six. It sticks tightly to the lining, where it gets nourishment via the mother's bloodstream.

At 12 days, the embryo is still just a clump of around a couple of thousand of cells. The various parts of its body start growing after the first 2 weeks. The embryo gets embedded into the wall of the womb as some more cells are starting to form the placenta. Placenta brings the mother's blood vessels right alongside to the baby and begins to produce a hormone, which can be detected by a pregnancy test. At this point in the mother's menstrual cycle, the uterus lining will be grown and is ready to support the baby. The cells of the embryo now multiply and begin to take on specific functions. This process is called "differentiation" which leads to various types of cells such as blood cells, nerve cells and kidney cells. It takes just 38 weeks for a fertilized egg to grow into a baby. It is called an embryo until about eight weeks

after fertilization and from then it is instead known as a fetus. The development of the embryo is called embryogenesis.

During the first week after fertilization, the blastocyst binds to the wall of the uterus (endometrium). This results in forming connections between the mother and the embryo including the umbilical cord. During the next couple of weeks the embryo's growth centers around an axis, which will further become the spine and the body parts like brain, spinal cord, heart, and gastrointestinal tract begin to form. Three weeks after fertilization, the various parts of the embryo start to form. Three layers of cells form, out of which all the different organs of the body will develop sequentially. Two folds grow and develop along the length of the embryo – these roll up to make the neural tube which eventually becomes the brain and spinal cord. Embryo's life-supporting system known as placenta, starts to work, delivering nourishment and taking waste products away.

Chemicals that are produced by the embryo stop the woman's menstrual cycle. Meanwhile, neurogenesis is underway, showing brain activity at about the sixth week and the heart will begin to beat around the same time. Limb buds start to appear where arms and legs will grow later. Organogenesis begins. During 6th to 8th week, myogenesis and neurogenesis progress so that the embryo gets the capability to move, the eyes begin to form followed by further organogenesis and growth continues. Simultaneously, hair has started to form along with all essential organs and facial features begin to develop. The head represents about one half of the embryo's axial length, and more than half of the embryo's mass. The brain develops into five areas. Tissue growth and formation occurs and develops into the vertebra and some other bones. The heart starts to beat and pump the blood throughout the body.

By the end of the 8th week (10th week of pregnancy), the most familiar embryonic stage is over, and the fetal stage begins. All the different parts of the body are in place. Fingers and toes form – the embryo now has fingerprints which are unique. Its head is still very large compared to its body – almost half its length. The brain is growing at about 100,000 new brain cells every minute. Mostly protected by the amniotic fluid, the fetus can move around and also flex its limbs. The growth continues and by end of 12th week, it can hear sounds and its skin is sensitive to touch. The fetus grows very quickly during weeks 13 to 16 – doubling in size from 5 to 10 cm. The face starts to form, and by 14 weeks the eyes can move and the eyelids stay closed until the final two months of pregnancy. Now, eventually the internal organs are in their final positions, the bones begin to harden gradually, although they remain flexible until after the baby has been born. By 20 weeks, the mother can feel the fetus movement. It has eyebrows and hair on its head and its entire body is covered with smooth, fine, downy hair. A greasy substance called vernix safeguards the skin. The fetus practices swallowing and digesting fluid, and can even recognize sweet tastes from bitter ones!

An ultrasound scan may now reveal whether the fetus is a boy or a girl. During the second half of pregnancy, the fetus becomes progressively aware of the outside world. It can be startled by sudden noises, and is thought to be enough capable of feeling pain after 5-6 months. Increased eye movements, associated with dreaming begin at 21 weeks. The fetus looks absolutely transparent, as it doesn't yet have any fat under its skin.

By 26 weeks, the lungs are ready, developed enough to control breathing and body temperature to some extent. It has eyelashes and fingernails, appears less wrinkled with more fat laid down under the skin. The baby's skin is now pink in color and smooth in texture, and its arms and legs are much fatter than before. The eyes open eventually, and by 30 weeks the pupils will dilate and contract in response to light. The mother may also feel the baby hiccupping, if it has swallowed too much amniotic fluid. By 34 weeks, most of the babies have their heads downwards, ready for birth in normal cases. The baby continues to put on weight, outgrowing the womb, and starts the birth off by releasing and synthesizing hormones. Finally, the muscles of the mother's womb start to contract, and labor begins. In most of the cases, babies are born within ten days of their due date.

Boy or a Girl?

In organisms, half of our genes come from our father and half come from our mother. They are bundled up as a set of 46 chromosomes. One pair of these known as the sex chromosomes determine the gender. An embryo with one X and one Y chromosome will be a boy, and one with two X-chromosomes will be a girl. The presence of a Y-chromosome turns on a 'male switch' in the developing embryo. In male embryos, the testis determining factor gene, called SRY, is then switched on. This 'male gene' on the Y-chromosome triggers male genital development and absence of Y-chromosome in female embryo allows ovaries and female genitals to develop.

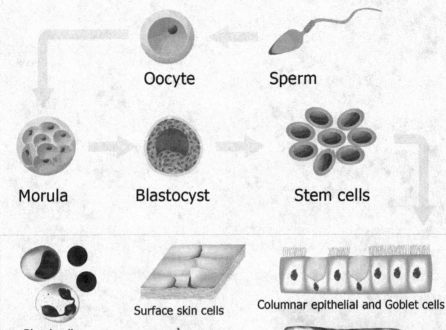

Oocyte

Sperm

Morula

Blastocyst

Stem cells

Blood cells

Surface skin cells

Columnar epithelial and Goblet cells

Bone cells

Cardiac muscle cells

Neuron

Skeletal muscle cells

Smooth muscle cells

Development of specialized cells

Baby

Transformation of a single cell into a baby

Chapter Five

The fourth miracle:
All life is one and
yet you are unique

How do you become you?

Your DNA and the genes in it define your nature. Both your environment and your genes influence the person you become. In the most literal and fundamental sense we are all family as we share our ancestors and most of us are related in some way or other. If you compare your genes with any other human being's they will be about 99.9 percent the same. The tiny differences in that remaining 0.1 percent – roughly one nucleotide base in every thousand – are what endow us with our individuality. It is the endless combination of our genomes – each nearly identical but not quite – that makes us what we are, both as individuals and as species.

Inside the cell is a nucleus, and inside each nucleus are the forty six little bundles of complex chromosomes. With very few exceptions, every cell in your body (99.999 percent of them) carries the same complement of chromosomes. Chromosomes constitute the complete set of instructions necessary to make and maintain you and are made of long strands of the little wonder chemical called deoxyribonucleic acid or DNA – the most extraordinary molecule on Earth! The shape of a DNA molecule is rather like a spiral staircase or twisted rope ladder: the famous double helix. The structure of DNA molecules is made up of a type of sugar called deoxyribose and the whole of the helix is a nucleic acid – hence the name deoxyribonucleic acid.

The DNA in the nucleus of human cell, a complex bio-molecule that defines you, measures about 2 yards which means there would be 125 billion miles of DNA in your physical body! Your own DNA then if uncoiled could wrap around the Earth 5 million times and that string could stretch to the Sun and back 400 times!! The instructions for the building of proteins are coded in the DNA. Proteins enable DNA to replicate using the data stored in the DNA itself. DNA was isolated in 1869, and over the next 50 years scientists gradually refined their understanding of the molecule. In 1953, James Watson and Francis Crick shook the scientific world with an elegant double-helical model for the structure of DNA.

Importance of DNA

DNA is an extremely important molecule for life on Earth. The genetic information in DNA is the basis of cell growth and development, division, and function. The resemblance of offspring to their parents has its basis in the precise replication of DNA and its transmission from one generation to the next. The arrangement of bases in a DNA molecule spells out the genetic code which determine the characteristics of the offspring. Hereditary information is encoded in the chemical language of DNA and reproduced in all the cells of our body. DNA directs the development of our physiological and behavioral traits.

Structure and Composition

Structurally, DNA is a double helix resembling a twisted ladder. DNA is formed with nucleotides which are structural units of DNA containing a base, a sugar and one or more phosphates. The four bases of DNA bases bond only with their complements (Adenine bonds with Thymine, and Cytosine bonds with Guanine). The bases are joined to one another in pairs by relatively weak chemical bonds called hydrogen bonds.

DNA acts as smart facsimile machine

Our cells need to divide, so we can grow and re-build. Every cell needs to have the instructions to know 'how to be' a cell. DNA provides those instructions – so a new copy of itself must be made before a cell divides. One side of the double-stranded DNA helix can be used as a template to produce a complement. The original strand and the new one combine together to form a new DNA double helix, which is identical to the original. Human DNA can unzip and 'replicate' at hundreds of places along the structure at the same time – speeding up the process for a very long molecule.

The ultimate hard drive

DNA exists for one reason – to create more DNA! And you have a lot of it inside you: about six feet of it squeezed into almost every cell nucleus which has a diameter of just five-thousandths of a millimeter. Each length of DNA comprises some 3.2 billion letters of coding and it would take more than five thousand average sized books to print that figure! Look at yourself in the mirror and reflect upon the fact that you are beholding hundred trillion cells and almost every one of those holds two yards of densely compacted DNA. According to one calculation, you may have as much as twenty million kilometers of DNA bundled up inside you. Your body, in short, loves to make DNA and without it you could not live.

Genes are made up of stretches of the DNA molecule which contain information about how to build proteins – the building blocks of life which make up everything about us. Different sequences of the four types of DNA bases make 'codes' which can be translated into amino

acids which are building blocks of proteins. Different combinations of amino acids produce at least 20,000 different proteins in the human body.

DNA Packaging

Each of us has enough DNA to reach from here to the Sun and again to back, more than 400 times approximately. How is all of that DNA packaged so tightly into chromosomes and squeezed into a tiny nucleus in the cell? The answer to this question lies in the fact that certain proteins compact chromosomal DNA into the microscopic space of the eukaryotic nucleus in the cell. These specific proteins are called histones, and the resulting association of DNA-protein complex is called chromatin. Histones provide the energy (mainly in the form of electrostatic interactions) to fold the DNA further and as a result, chromatin can be packaged into a much smaller volume than DNA alone. Histones are a group of small, positively charged proteins termed H1, H2A, H2B, H3, and H4. As

DNA is negatively charged due to the presence of phosphate groups in its phosphate-sugar backbone, histones can bind easily with DNA very tightly. The basic repeating structural (and functional) unit of chromatin is the nucleosome that contains nine histone proteins and about 166 base pairs of DNA. Every chromosome contains hundreds of thousands of nucleosomes and all these are joined by the DNA that runs between them (an average of about 20 base pairs). This joining segment of DNA is referred to as linker DNA. Each chromosome is thus a long chain of nucleosomes that gives the appearance of a string of beads when viewed using an electron microscope.

Genes define you

Genes are pieces of DNA – a code that sets down the order of the amino acids in a protein. Genes are instructions to make proteins and putting all these genes together you have the great symphony of existence known as the human genome. The genome is a kind of 'instruction manual' for the body. The genome,

as Eric Lander of MIT has put it, is like a 'parts list' for the human body.

You have 3.2 billion nucleotide base pairs of DNA in almost every one of your cells, but only about 3% of it makes up genes. Of the remaining 97%, some help in keeping the DNA bound together. Scientists used to call this 'junk DNA'. Now they have found that much non-coding DNA has essential roles such as controlling the activity of genes. Nearly every cell in your body contains the same set of around 24,000 genes.

Gene regulation and expression

Each new cell in the growing embryo receives a full set of genes and each cell must end up in the right place, doing the right job. Some genes are instructions for proteins that regulate the activity of other genes. Such 'control genes' govern important events in the developing embryo. Your body needs to make some proteins throughout your life whereas others are only needed at certain times. So genes are regulated so that cells make the right amount of protein, just at the time when it is needed. Proteins made by a particular cell depend on the location of the cell in the embryo, age of the embryo and the instructions it receives from its own genes and from other cells.

Genes generally express their functional effect through the production of proteins, which are responsible for most of the functions in the cell. Proteins are formed by a sequence of amino acids, and the DNA sequence of a gene (through an RNA intermediate) is used to produce a specific protein sequence. Codon is a sequence of three nucleotides in the sequence and corresponds to one of the twenty possible amino acids in protein – this correspondence is called the genetic code.

The genes make sure the correct body parts grow in the right place – your head at the top of your body and feet at the bottom. The embryo must know its left from its right before the organs start to grow and genes control this. Hox (Hoemeotic) genes are 'master switches', which switch other genes on and off. They answered the long bewildering

question of how billions of embryonic cells, all arising from a single fertilized egg and carrying identical DNA know where to go and what to do – whether it should become a liver cell, a neuron or a blood cell. As we already know, all the cells in our body started from a single cell. This particular single cell divides many times to turn into trillion of cells and almost all the cells in our body share the same DNA as was found in that first cell. If all the cells in the human body have the same DNA, then why don't all our cells function the same way? Why the functioning of our eyes and lungs is so different? The answer lies with the expression of genes in the DNA. The functioning of cell is related to the synthesis of proteins which in turn depends on the expression of genes. The proteins then perform some set of specific tasks and functions in the cells where they are made. For example, hemoglobin, a protein found in RBCs, carries oxygen to cells and carbon dioxide away and millions of these hemoglobin proteins shall be carried by RBC to all other cells for them to function properly. Lungs and eyes are so different because different sets of proteins are made in the various lung and eye cells. In the eye, particular kind of genes is turned on for seeing and the "breathing" genes are off. In lung cells, the situation will be reversed. Even though DNA contains lots of recipes, only those required to make and run an eye are used in an eye. Some exceptions are: RBC are without DNA and the gametes (sperms and eggs) have half the number of chromosomes.

The embryonic cells have different functions and form three layers: The outer layer (ectoderm) grows into skin, brain and nerves. The middle layer (mesoderm) grows into blood vessels, muscle and many of the organs. The inner layer (endoderm) grows into the gut, stomach and lungs. The three layers of cells form the structures that will eventually make all the different parts of the body. The neural tube develops a structure that will eventually form the brain and spinal cord.

How you are unique from others?

You are genetically distinct from your parents and this genetic variation lies in the behavior of chromosomes, DNA in chromosomes and the genes in DNA. Inheritance of traits such as color of eyes, skin and hair, facial features and overall physical appearance arises out of tens of thousands of genes we inherit from our parents. The coded information in the form of genes programs the specific traits that we inherit, and DNA contains this coded information in the form of specific sequence of nucleotides. The sequence of coded words program cells to synthesize specific enzymes and other proteins whose cumulative action produces an organism's inherited traits.

There are two main processes during sexual reproduction; the first one is meiosis, involving the halving of the number of chromosomes; and fertilization which involves the fusion of two gametes and the restoration of the original number of chromosomes. In the first stage of reproduction, in meiosis, the number of chromosomes is reduced from a diploid number (2n) to a haploid number (n). During "fertilization", haploid gametes come together to form a diploid zygote and the original number of chromosomes (2n) is restored. During fertilization, one "gamete" from each parent combines to form a "zygote". Because of recombination and independent assortment phenomena in meiosis, each gamete contains a different set of DNA. This specifically produces a unique combination of genes in the resulting zygote.

Independent assortment and recombination allow for a greater diversity of genotypes in the population. Each of the homologous pairs of chromosomes may orient with either its maternal or paternal homologue closer to a given pole during the process of cell division into gametes. Thus, there is a 50% chance that a particular daughter cell of meiosis will get the maternal chromosome of a certain homologous pair and a 50% chance that it will receive the paternal chromosome. This reshuffling of genes into unique combinations increases the genetic variation in a population and explains the variation we see between siblings with the same parents. Thus, meiosis helps to generate improved variety,

and results in incredible diversity of life on Earth.

Independent assortment

Independent assortment causes genetic diversity as the chromosomes supplied by one's parents are literally independently assorted into resulting gametes. It is achieved when chromosomes line up in homologous pairs and move independently to the opposite poles during anaphase stage of meiosis (process for cell division into gametes). The process is governed by complex enzyme systems which in turn must also have come about by chance phenomenon. The most possible variation that can be achieved by independent assortment depends on the number of chromosomes present in the organisms. In humans, there are 46 chromosomes, which will arrange themselves in 23 homologous pairs.

If we inherit our parents 'genes', then why don't we look exactly like them? If the complete 23 pairs inherit as it is to the child, he or she will look exactly like his father or mother, but what actually happens is – the genes randomly pass to the next generation. Due to this, even siblings inherit very different chromosomal combinations. From each parent, there are 2^{23} possible combinations. There are thus 80 trillion possible variations. This variation is increased even further when two gametes unite during fertilization, thus creating offspring with unique DNA combinations.

Recombination

Meiosis also produces genetic variation by way of the process of recombination which is also referred as crossing over. The chromosomes of each pair usually cross over to achieve homologous recombination. The pairing of homologous chromosomes at prophase I is different than the pairing that occurs between complementary strands of DNA. The DNA of non-sister chromatids becomes aligned and when both a maternal copy and a paternal copy of homologues pair line up against each other. The two homologues swap genetic material in a process

called crossing over producing recombinant chromosomes. There can be multiple crossovers between non-sister chromatids. Furthermore, crossover configurations can occur in any combination and can lead to dramatically different outcomes.

Crossing over occurs at different points along the chromosome and every meiotic process need not involve crossing over in the same set of genes each time. There is at least one crossover per homologous pair and the homologues are now different than the parents' chromosomes. So, each of them may carry a different set of genetic information.

Many factors affect crossing over and it is not possible to predict the location where crossing over occurs. It is a chance event as the break points on the DNA sequence of the chromosomes are random. The probability of crossing over between genes on a chromosome is dependent on the distances between the genes. This process is a source of genetic recombination and produces recombinant chromosomes.

Mutation vs Variation

Mutations are the changes in DNA sequence. Mutations lead to genetic variation by producing random changes in genetic code of an organism. Usually DNA mutations give a negative effect and this mainly results in not producing important proteins or enzymes. So the organism cannot do certain things (eg: not digesting fats, not having enough strength to fight against diseases etc). But sometimes DNA mutations lead to better variety of organisms. This is known as positive effect of DNA mutations. In this phenomenon, survival is more likely and the mutated (beneficial) gene is passed on to it's offspring. Many living things on Earth are here because of successful mutations, but many have gone extinct due to harmful mutations. Over time, mutations occur (sometimes random) in order to assist a species to survive. Thus, genetic variation is useful because it helps populations change over time. Genetic variations that help an organism survive and reproduce are passed on to the next generation. Each person has a unique genome, causing individual phenotypic variations such as physical appearance. Individual variation occurs in populations of all species and this is only due to diversity phenomenon. In human beings, for example, the enormous variety of people's faces reflects each person's genetic individuality. Thus, **you and me are unique in our own way!**

Chapter Six

The fifth miracle:
Your body and brain

Body – a network of trillions of loosely coupled, self organized cells with shared intelligence and a shared goal to keep you alive.

Your body is a complex system integrating a number of biological systems that carry out specific functions necessary for everyday living. The system as whole regulates its internal environment and maintains a stable condition required for the body to function effectively so that you survive. The nervous system, endocrine system, digestive system, respiratory system, circulatory system, immune system, urinary system, reproductive system and others work together through the vital organs (brain, heart, lungs, kidneys) and trillions of cells they are made of with incredible precision, exactly the way they should. We can't survive even if one essential enzyme or hormone is missing or malfunctions.

Let us review how some of the systems work. The nervous system consists of the central nervous system (the brain and spinal cord) and the peripheral nervous system.

The brain is the organ of thought and sensory processing (vision, hearing, taste, and smell). The brain enables communication and control of various other systems and functions. The average human brain has about 100 billion nerve cells called neurons. The nervous system controls both voluntary actions and involuntary actions by sending signals to different parts of the body.

The circulatory system or cardiovascular system comprises the heart and blood vessels (arteries, veins, and capillaries). The human heart is responsible for pumping blood throughout our body. The heart propels the circulation of the blood and through blood it transports oxygen, nutrients, immune cells and hormones. The circulatory system which consists of the heart, blood vessels and blood plays an important role in fighting diseases and maintaining homeostasis (proper temperature and pH balance). Your heart beats about 100,000 times per day, sending about 7500 liters of blood through your body. Your heart which is about the size of your fist pumps blood through 60,000 miles of blood vessels that feed your organs and tissues. The capillaries, which are the smallest of the blood vessels, would constitute nearly 80 percent of this length. By comparison, the circumference of the Earth is about 25,000 miles (40,000 km) which means that your blood vessels could wrap around the planet nearly 2.5 times! The circulatory system's main function is to transport blood, nutrients, gases and hormones to and from the cells throughout the body. Blood leaves the left side of the heart and flows through arteries and then into capillaries where food and oxygen are released to the body cells, while carbon dioxide and other waste products are returned to the bloodstream. The blood travels in veins back to the right side of the heart and from there it is pumped to the lungs.

The respiratory system which takes oxygen from air and leaves carbon dioxides back into air, consists of the nose, trachea, and lungs. The lungs contain over 300,000 million capillaries which are tiny blood vessels and if they were laid end-to-end, they would stretch 1500 miles. The lungs are responsible for removing oxygen from the air we breathe and transferring it to our blood where it can be sent to our cells. Red blood cells collect the oxygen from the lungs and carry it to the parts of the body where it is needed. They collect the carbon dioxide and transport it back to the lungs. We exhale carbon dioxide which is removed by the lungs. A complete lack of oxygen is known as anoxia and a decrease in oxygen levels is known as hypoxia. Hypoxia for about five minutes leads to destruction of brain cells and may cause brain damage and ultimately death.

The endocrine system consists of glands which secrete different types of hormones for regulating vital functions such as metabolism, reproduction, growth and development. The word endocrine derives from the Greek words "endo," meaning within, and "crinis," meaning secrete. The most common endocrine disease is diabetes, a condition in which the body does not properly process glucose. The endocrine system consists of eight major glands, which produce and secrete chemicals called hormones. These hormones, in turn, travel to different tissues and regulate various bodily functions, such as metabolism, growth and development. The urinary system includes kidneys, ureters, the bladder and the urethra. The job of the kidneys is to remove waste and extra fluid from the blood. The kidneys remove urea – waste product formed by the breakdown of proteins – from the blood through small filtering units called nephrons. Human kidneys have about 1 million nephrons that filter out liquids and wastes. Each day, the kidneys process about 50 gallons of blood and filter an average of around 1.3 liters of blood per minute.

The digestive system converts food into energy and growth molecules which nourish the body which are circulated to all tissues of the body and excretes the unused residue. The human digestive system is a series of organs that converts food into essential nutrients that are absorbed into the body and moves the unused waste material out of the body. The majority of the absorption of nutrients occurs in small intestine.

The immune system consists of the white blood cells, the thymus and the lymph nodes. It provides a mechanism for the body to distinguish its own cells from alien cells and substances. The immune system neutralizes or destroys the foreign bodies by using specialized proteins such as antibodies, cytokines, and toll-like receptors. It protects us from bacteria, viruses and other pathogens that may be harmful. Lymphocytes, the small white blood cells play a large role in defending the body against disease. Leukocytes identify and eliminate pathogens and are considered as the second arm of the innate immune system. The innate leukocytes include macrophages, neutrophils, dendritic cells, and natural killer cells. Each of your cells has a set of 'identity tags' called antigens and the set of antigens is unique for every person. Your immune system recognizes invading germs such as bacteria and viruses because they have unfamiliar antigens on their surfaces. It uses a huge army of defender cells – different types of white blood cells. You make about millions of them every day in your bone marrow and some of these cells, called macrophages destroy germs as soon as they enter. This is your 'natural' or inborn immunity. T-cells and B-cells are highly specialized defender cells which fight the infection. B-cells make antibodies that attack bacteria and toxins and T-cells help destroy infected or cancerous cells. Killer T-cells kill cells that are infected with viruses and other pathogens. Helper T-cells help determine which immune responses the body makes to a particular pathogen. Thymus is an organ where T-cells mature. With the help of T-cells, B-cells make special Y-shaped proteins called antibodies. Antibodies stick to antigens on the surface of germs and patrolling defender cells called phagocytes engulf and destroy antibody-covered intruders.

Metabolism and Homeostasis

Metabolism and Homeostasis are the two important functions the body performs to sustain our life. Each of these functions can be performed effectively only if all the constituent biological systems work in harmony. The body does everything that is required to be done 24 hours a day, and 7 days a week to deliver the right molecules in the right amount, to the right place and at the right time to make sure you maintain the balance. You do not have to consciously direct this and everything happens on its own most of the time.

Brain

Your brain is a hub of 100 billion neurons with more than 100 trillion connections. The nervous system is a network of cells called neurons. Human brain weighs about three pounds which constitutes about two percent of the body weight but it is six times larger relative to the body size. The increase in brain size was accomplished by way of brain folding which hides most of its gray matter and material within the folds. The tissue of the brain can be broken down into gray matter and white matter. Gray matter region consists of mostly interneurons with areas of nerve connections and processing. White matter is made of mostly myelinated neurons that connect the regions of gray matter as the information highway of the brain to speed the connections between distant parts of the brain and body. The brain is broadly divided into three regions: forebrain (also called neo-cortex or cerebral cortex), midbrain and hindbrain (brain stem and cerebellum). Each of them is different in shape, size, structure and functionality. Each one of them works independently but the whole brain works together to make the sum greater than parts.

Forebrain

The forebrain consists mainly of cerebrum and diencephalon. The cerebral cortex forms the outermost part of the cerebrum, consisting of six parallel layers of neurons running tangential to the brain surface. The cerebral cortex (also called neocortex) is less than 5 mm thick but has a large surface area of about 0.5 m^2 and accounts for about 80% of total brain mass. The neo cortex is also divided into right hemisphere and left hemisphere, each of which is responsible for the opposite half of the body. The cerebral cortex controls voluntary movement and cognitive functions. Each side of the cerebral cortex is customarily described as having four lobes, called the frontal, temporal, occipital and parietal lobes. There are number of functional areas within each lobe. These areas include primary sensory areas, which receive and process a specific type of sensory information and association areas, which integrate the information from various parts of the brain.

The frontal lobes are responsible for intentional action and are associated with executive functions such as self-awareness and abstract thought. They coordinate almost all the functions in the rest of the brain. The parietal lobes are feeling and sensing regions of the cortex which process what we feel and the information we receive from body like pressure, temperature, vibration, pain and touch. The feel and sensations in various parts of the body are mapped in the somatosensory areas located in the parietal lobes.

The temporal lobes process sounds, smell, perception, learning, language and memory. The electrical signals we receive from the ear drum fire neurons in the temporal lobe. The combination, sequence and the location of neural circuits is processed to provide meaning when we listen to music, have a conversation, watch television and anything else related to hearing. The temporal lobes help us recognize the previous experiences, familiarity and also find meaning in the visual symbols. They are responsible for language, hearing, conceptual thinking and associative memories.

The occipital lobes manage visual information and interpret visual qualities like light, movement, form, shape, depth and color. The visual information is processed in six different regions of occipital lobes and they are all integrated to form a picture that is communicated to temporal lobes which in turn provide meaning to this visual information.

Most sensory information coming into the cortex is directed via the thalamus to primary sensory areas within the lobes: visual information to the occipital lobe; auditory input to the temporal lobe; and somatosensory information to the parietal lobe. The primary sensory areas send information to nearby association areas that can process particular features in the sensory input. Based on the integrated sensory information, the cerebral cortex may generate motor commands that cause specific behaviors. These commands consist of action potentials produced by neurons in the primary motor cortex. The action potentials travel along axons to the brainstem and spinal cord, where they excite motor neurons, which in turn excite skeletal muscle cells.

Epithalamus, thalamus and hypo-thalamus are three important regions in diencephalon (interbrain). The epithalamus includes the pineal gland and the choroid plexus that produce cerebrospinal fluid from blood. The pineal gland, a tiny, pine cone-shaped structure secrets different neurotransmitters like serotonin and melatonin depending on the amount of light the eyes receive, to regulate our cycles of sleep and wakefulness. The thalamus and hypothalamus are major integrating centers. The former is like a central junction point which acts as the main input center for sensory information going to the cerebrum and the main output center for motor information leaving the cerebrum. The information received from all the senses is sorted in the thalamus and sent to the appropriate cerebral centers for further processing. The thalamus is also a relay point between the neocortex and the brainstem. It also signals the hypothalamus to chemically prepare your fight-or-flight body functions, so that our body has the energy to respond to the threat. The pear shaped pituitary gland, which hangs off the hypothalamus like a fruit, secretes chemicals to communicate with body's other major glands and activate various hormonal states.

The hypothalamus, which weighs only a few grams, is one of the most important brain regions for homeostatic regulation. It generates chemical messengers called neuropeptides to regulate the body's internal environment, to balance and adapt to the changes in external environment. It also contains the body's thermostat, as well as centers to control and manage hunger, thirst, sleep, blood sugar levels, heart rate, blood pressure, hormonal balance, immune system, metabolism and many other basic survival mechanisms. Hypothalamus generates hormones that make you feel the way you are just thinking or how you are reacting.

Midbrain

The midbrain region located near the very center of the brain between the interbrain and the hindbrain is composed of a portion of the brainstem, hippocampus, amygdala and basal ganglia. Hippocampus makes long-term memories by storing information involved with our experiences as associative memory that we may like to access in future. Amygdala which means "almond-shaped" is responsible for alerting the body in survival situations, sometimes as precognitive response. It is also associated with the storage of memories involving emotions such as fear, anger, sadness and joy and with the perception of certain situations based on those memories. The basal ganglia are intricate bundles of neurological networks located under the neocortex with connections to neocortex to integrate thoughts and feelings with physical actions, fine tune motor movement (ex: riding a bicycle), control anxiety and enhance feelings of pleasure.

Hindbrain

The hindbrain consists of the remaining brainstem as well as our cerebellum and pons. The cerebellum or little brain is important for coordination and error checking during motor, perceptual and cognitive functions. It is likely involved in learning and remembering motor skills. The cerebellum integrates this sensory and motor information as it coordinates movements and balance. Attitudes, repeated actions, conditioned behaviors, emotional reactions, reflexes and skills that

we have mastered are all embedded in the cerebellum. The neurons in cerebellum, called Purkinje's cells, process between 100,000 to one million connections per neuron and more than half of the neurons in human brain are part of cerebellum. The cerebellum is the most densely packed area of gray matter in the brain.

The medulla oblongata, simply called the medulla, is the lowest portion of the brain located at the base of the skull. It is roughly triangular and is continued behind as the spinal cord. Its function is to control the activities of the internal organs and several visceral functions for example, peristaltic movement of the alimentary canal, movement of breathing, beating of heart, blood vessel activity and many other involuntary actions. The pons also participate in some of these activities, like regulating the breathing centers in the medulla.

Brain Stem

The brainstem plays a vital role in homeostasis and coordination of movement. Several centers in the brainstem contain neuron cell bodies that send axons to many areas of the cerebral cortex and cerebellum, releasing neurotransmitters such as norepinephrine, dopamine, serotonin and acetylcholine.

All axons carrying sensory information to brain and motor instructions from higher brain regions pass through the brainstem, making information transmission one of the most important functions of the medulla and pons. Most of the axons carrying instructions about movement from the midbrain and forebrain to the spinal cord cross from one side of the CNS to the other in the medulla. As a result, the right side of the brain controls much of the movement of the left side of the body, and left side of the brain controls movement of the right side of the body.

Growth and development of Brain

Once the embryo has marked out its future brain and spinal cord, 4000 new neurons are produced per second approximately. The embryo also makes glial cells which provide support to neurons and guide and glue the electrical communication networks of neurons. Neural tube is formed around the groove running along the length of the embryo. The nerve cell factory in the developing embryo is the lining of the neural tube, which forms both the brain and spinal cord. Three different compartments start to grow at the head end of the tube, which will become the forebrain, midbrain and hindbrain. After birth, your brain continues to grow and develops as you grow up.

The embryo produces many more neurons than it needs to ensure that all possible connections can be established and there will never be too few. The neurons that get to the right place and successfully make connections survive. Once an area of the brain has enough connections, any others growing towards the same point will die by switching on a 'cell suicide program' – apoptosis. A baby's brain develops through experiences, gained during certain periods of its development. The more experiences a child has, the more connections its brain cells will make.

Neurons that fire together wire together. As we repeat the same actions and thoughts, from practicing a tennis serve to playing a piano, certain neural connections become more fixed in the brain and your brain changes with each passing year getting rewired with new connections. We have been adapting, learning, making memories and becoming smart and wiser (hopefully) with real life experiences. There are of course less desirable changes like loss of memory, agility and responsiveness due to loss of neurons and it happens to every one of us.

Nervous System

The nervous system is a highly specialized network, which responds to external stimuli such as viewing a football match and responds through physiological changes such as increase of adrenaline in the system and increase of one's heartbeat along with the sense of excitement. The nervous system works by controlling and co-ordinating activities for homeostasis and metabolism. It controls both voluntary and involuntary actions. You use your senses to gather information about the outside world. All the sensations that arise out of sensory inputs change into electrical signals and carried to your brain which then puts all the information together to produce the whole picture.

The human nervous system consists of the central nervous system (CNS) and the peripheral nervous system (PNS). The CNS consisting of brain and spinal cord is the largest part of the nervous system. CNS is derived from the dorsal embryonic nerve cord, which is hollow. This feature persists as the narrow central canal of the spinal cord and the four ventricles of the brain. The central canal as well as the ventricles are filled with cerebrospinal fluid that circulates slowly through the central canal and ventricles and then drains into the veins. It facilitates supply of nutrients and hormones to different parts of the brain and the removal of wastes. The cerebrospinal fluid also cushions the brain and spinal cord.

The PNS consists of the nerves and ganglia outside of the brain and spinal cord. The main function of the PNS is to connect the CNS to the limbs and organs. The PNS is divided into the somatic nervous system and the autonomic nervous system. The somatic system is responsible for transmission of motor and sensory information between CNS and the sensory organs as well as skeletal muscles. The somatic system processes sensory information received from external stimuli such as sight, hearing and touch and affects voluntary muscle movements. There are three parts to your autonomic nervous system – sympathetic system ('fight-or-flight' reaction), parasympathetic system (controls heart rate and body temperature under normal conditions) and the enteric system (controls the workings of your gut).

Neurons and Glial cells

The nervous system is made up of neurons which are interconnected to each other in complex arrangements and communicate through electrochemical signals. The nervous system uses a mixture of electrical and chemical signals to send messages at a faster rate. Sensory neurons carry impulses from a receptor to the CNS. Motor neurons carry impulses from the CNS to an effector. Relay neurons, also called interneurons, transmit impulses between the sensory and motor neurons. There are ten times as many glial cells than neurons and they look after the structure and maintenance of the brain but do not actually conduct electrical impulses. Glial cells provide support and protection for neurons and are thus known as the "glue" of the nervous system. The four main functions of glial cells are to hold neurons in their place, to supply nutrients and oxygen to neurons, to insulate neurons from one another, to destroy pathogens and to remove dead neurons.

Astrocytes, oligodendrocytes, microglia, and ependymal cells are different types of glial cells. Astrocytes protect neurons by filtering nutrients out of the blood and preventing chemicals and pathogens from leaving the capillaries of the brain. Oligodendrocytes produce myelin which insulates axons and accelerate the communication speed. Microglia attacks and destroys pathogens that invade the brain. Ependymal cells line the capillaries of the choroid plexuses and filter blood plasma to produce cerebrospinal fluid.

Neurons are the building blocks of the nervous system and the information travels along neurons as electrical signals – nerve impulses. These signals are passed at special sites known as synapses – the junctions between two neurons. Action potential is transmitted from one neuron to a neighboring one at the narrow gap (about 20nm in width) between the neurons called the synaptic cleft. Neurons coordinate multiple functions in organisms by sending messages that travel at a usual pace of 100 meters per second.

All neurons have the same basic parts. The 'control centre' of the cell is known as the cell body. The axon (nerve fibre) transmits electrical signals from the cell body. The branching fibres called dendrites receive electrical signals from other neurons. The electrical signals (nerve impulses) carried by neurons are passed on to other neurons at the synapses. Each neuron communicates with many others and this contributes to the amazing complexity of the brain. Chemical signaling is far more versatile and uses over fifty different types of neurotransmitters. When a nerve impulse reaches the synapse at the end of a neuron, it triggers the neuron to release a neurotransmitter. The neurotransmitter moves across the gap between the neurons and on reaching the target neuron, fits into a receptor on the surface of the target neuron, like a key in a lock. This process converts the chemical signal back into an electrical nerve impulse. The signals carried by some neurotransmitters excite the target cell while others dampen down their activity. The response depends on the type of neurotransmitter and the receptors they reach.

We can see from the above facts that trillions and trillions of entities namely cells, molecules and their associated activities occur with incredible precision to help you and me to be alive and just be humans.

Chapter Seven

The flow of life

Those who flow as life flows know they need no other force.

– Lao Tzu

The question "Who am I?" bothered me many times. When I asked this question, the most genuine answer from most of the people who really reflected and pondered over was that there can only be pointers to the truth. They suggested paths to realize the truth but every individual has to necessarily walk the path to experience it. "It can't be explained and can only be experienced" is the typical suggestion to the seeker.

Some of us who identify the concept of "I" with body and mind find both of them changing all the time. We tend to be perplexed about the "I" that could possibly remain constant over time and in trying to find that tend to identify ourselves with something beyond body and mind. This curiosity led many people to explore various schools of thought propounded by many philosophers in this short human history. They seem to be comfortable in identifying the self with spirit which is considered eternal but they are not really sure as they could not experience it. Scientific investigations in this direction have not conclusively proved anything

that can be verified objectively within the framework of body and mind.

The enlightened ones showed the path to experience the truth and millions continue to walk the path suggested by them. The author however proposes a different paradigm to investigate, comprehend, analyze, synthesize, experience and evaluate from a scientific perspective which may be helpful only to the extent of gaining intellectual understanding. The experiential wisdom gained by walking the path suggested by enlightened ones can only lead to liberation – freedom from our conditioned mind.

We have briefly explored the five miracles to understand who we are and how we come to exist and if there is anything in particular that we can identify with – beyond the process going on continuously within our body and mind. We come to understand that our planet Earth itself is a tiny speck in this vast Universe with billions of galaxies and trillions of stars. You and me, as individuals, would be like dots in this world with billions of humans and trillions of living beings existing right now on our planet Earth. There are many things which happened exactly the right way for the Universe to evolve giving birth to galaxies, stars and planets. Earth is a rare planet with right conditions for sustenance of life. Many more amazing events occurred in the evolution of life from microbes to intelligent humans. We should be really grateful for being so lucky that inconceivable number of events occurred with such great precision leading to the evolution of Universe in which we exist - birth of planet Earth with conditions suitable for life and the evolution of life giving birth to human beings. This understanding provides the context and a perspective of our place in this Universe.

Human body is a testimony to the incredible engineering prowess of Mother Nature. Trillions of tiny components inside the body act in perfect unison to realize a larger goal. It is like a very well choreographed ballet where each one in the play knows as to what his or her role is and when he/she needs to spring into action for the other person's act to be consummated. Everything happens with incredible precision followed by a series of complex processes, of which many of them happen without any conscious direction from their own mind. It is more than a miracle that trillions of tiny parts called cells within you are working and talking to each other with great precision and exactly the way they should, so that you can read this, comprehend and wonder about our essential nature.

Some of the amazing things we find about ourselves, our body and mind are:

You are stardust and most of it is empty inside

The components of your body are truly ancient: you are stardust as the atoms in your body were produced initially from the Big Bang 13.7 billion years ago. It is hard to grasp just how small the atoms that make up your body are until you take a look at the sheer number of them. An adult is made up of around 7,000,000,000,000,000,000,000,000,000 (7 octillion) atoms. The atoms that make up your body are mostly empty space. If there is no empty space you would compress into a tiny, tiny volume. For example, in a hydrogen atom the empty space is about 99.999999999999%.

One in all, all in one

You find your DNA, which defines in a way who you are, in each and every cell; the way each and every part of your body grows and functions is defined in every single strand of DNA. Billions of neurons in your brain connect and communicate with trillions of cells spread over various parts of your body through electrical signals and chemical signals called neurotransmitters. The breath which keeps you alive connects everything else and oxygenates trillions of cells. The oxygen is circulated through red blood cells and your heart pumps blood through 60,000 miles of blood vessels that feed your organs and tissues, which is about 2.5 times the circumference of the Earth. The oxygen is taken up by

the mitochondria which are cell's "power stations" and there are about a thousand of them in a typical cell. Mitochondria convert food and oxygen you take, into ATP, which keeps you going. So, all the parts and cells in your body are connected influencing the functioning of other parts.

Change is the only constant

Everything in our body changes at every level – subatomic, atomic, molecular and cellular. According to popular physicist and noble laureate Richard P Feynman, protons interact with themselves in many ways and the simplest proton self-interaction is the emission and re-absorption of a virtual pion within the time permitted by 'uncertainty principle'. Proton also may emit a positive pion, momentarily transforming itself into neutron and back into a proton again. Neutrons too, like electrons and protons, constantly interact with themselves by emitting and re-absorbing virtual particles.

All particles exist potentially, with a certain degree of probability, as different combinations of other particles and each combination has a certain probability of happening. The appearance of physical reality is based upon the interdependence of all things. In the subatomic realm there is no such thing as empty space. A type of Feynman diagram called 'vacuum diagram' depicts an exquisite dance of emptiness becoming form and form becoming emptiness. These transformations occur continuously in the subatomic realm and are limited only by the uncertainty principle, the conservation laws and probability.

The understanding of nature at quantum level helps us look at our self through the same lens and see the transient nature of the constituents of "I" leading to impermanence at every level. We are made of atoms which in turn are made up of nucleons (protons and neutrons). Proton is made up of quarks, lots of gluons and quark-antiquark pairs flying around at nearly the speed of light. They are held together by the strong nuclear force. They whizz around constantly colliding with each other and

converting one to another. The mass of nucleons comes from the motion-energy of a nucleon's quarks, anti-quarks and gluons and from the interaction energy of the strong nuclear forces that hold a nucleon intact. The cosmos, our planet Earth, our bodies and our breath are a result of inconceivable wild dance going on all the time. This amazing dance of life with trillions of events happening in our body, exactly the way they should with perfect orchestration, defines what we are.

Regeneration of cells and apoptosis

The human body contains nearly 100 trillion cells. Trillions of molecular and intra cellular reactions take place in our body every moment and the body will be replacing about one million cells per second. Most cells in our organs and tissues are continuously renewed. The cells lining the stomach replace themselves about every five days while cells in the epidermis last about a week and the red blood cells live for approximately four months in the body.

Most living cells seldom last more than a month with the exception of liver cells and brain cells. So, at the cellular level we are all youngsters as most of us are continuously replenished with new cells. The cells die in a dignified manner when they are no longer needed and this process is known as apoptosis or "programmed cell death". Billions of your cells die every day and billions of others clean up the mess. If cells do not die and begin to proliferate wildly, we call the result cancer. The body has elaborate mechanisms for dealing with it and it is only very rarely that the process spirals out of control. Humans suffer on an average one fatal malignancy for each 100 million billion cell divisions and hence it should really be a very rare occurrence.

So, who am I?

We could see that you and me are a sort of miracle in so many infinite ways and just cannot afford to miss a moment of wonderful life we are so blessed with. We can live our lives with joy and happiness as long as we are aware of the present moment with the understanding that there is no "me" inside our brain but for ever changing set of brain states. Walter J Freeman, an American biologist and a neuroscientist suggests in his article "Consciousness, Intentionality and causality" that circular causality is more relevant than linear causality in explaining the relationship between consciousness and neural activity. So "I" represents an ever changing set of brain states, a distillation of history, emotion, instinct, experience and the influence of other people and even chance. The insights we gain from being aware of the reality within and without is likely to dissolve our delusion of considering ourselves as something we can identify with, as something eternal that remains constant over a period of time, while the essential reality about "self" is similar to a flow where everything is changing every moment.

"I" is an ever changing flow of energy constantly evolving through an infinite variety of forms, shapes, thoughts, feelings of the knower, the known and the process of knowing itself. This understanding about

80

the essential nature of "self" as a flow of life rather than an eternal being will be helpful to reduce the self inflicted suffering from defilements associated with ego such as anger, greed, ill will and hatred. We become grateful to nature and happier in our lives while making this world a better place to live with peace, harmony and happiness. The wisdom lies in learning to live: being in the present moment of the flow and just being happy right now with this wonderful life.

Self awareness is likely to help us develop a sense of gratitude, let go of the past, stop worrying about the future and finally learn to live and enjoy the present moment in our life. This awareness is likely to free our mind from the not so healthy delusion about our identity which prevents us from living in the present moment. The reflection on the question "Who am I?" plays a vital role in providing meaning and direction to one's life. This would ultimately help people lead happy lives while leaving this world a better place than what they inherited. It is very important to understand that we are very lucky beyond comprehension and the least we can do is just be grateful to the 'Nature' and circumstances that lead to our existence as we are today!

The flow of life

The innate intelligence of our mind associated with our brain and body manages everything that keeps life flowing with our heart beating without interruption for about 100,000 times a day without our conscious involvement. The proteins read the sequence of DNA and produce more proteins required by the body. We can't read the DNA without proteins and we can't make proteins without DNA. The most interesting aspect in the flow of life is that from the union of just two cells, the life force creates 100 trillion specialized cells, regenerates that life and manages an inconceivable number of processes with incredible precision. Everything is changing every moment and in a couple of seconds nearly ten million cells are replaced and about 100,000 chemical reactions take place in each and every one of those 100 trillion cells that make up your body.

We can safely conclude from the above facts that life is extra-ordinary and change is the only constant in our body as well as mind. Mind is brain in action and is the product of consciousness that influences neural networks in the brain. It is more like the software, the intelligence, the consciousness which runs on its own unique operating system but pervades throughout the body including the brain as well as trillions of cells which constitute our body. We are like a flowing river and not like a rock. Our body and mind are more like a process than a structure, as almost everything in our body including structure of our brain changes continuously. Mitosis and apoptosis (cell division and cell death) give birth to a new "you and me" continuously and not a single moment can pass without some change or other. There is continuity with change and change with continuity within the framework of the body and mind. You and me represent the flow of life as a process – more as a verb than a noun.

Experience the flow with mindfulness

We can explore the truth about ourselves through mindfulness without depending on abstract conceptualization that lacks authentic experience. Brain has the capacity to create new neural connections and grow new neurons in response to thoughts and experience and hence mind can change the structure of the brain and relationships. The pattern of thoughts keep changing based on our experiences which shape the flow of energy. The mind is the process that regulates this flow of energy and information by observing and monitoring across time and also by modifying the same. The consciousness which enables us to think, be aware, perceive the world around us, maintain our free will and express ourselves as thinking, unique and individual self, is also changing all the time by learning, memorizing, creating, choosing, reacting and not reacting to the experiences in our interaction with the external world and within ourselves. The subconscious mind or the innate intelligence however directs millions of automatic functions at cellular and aggregate levels to keep us alive even without our conscious voluntary involvement.

Mindfulness or awareness is a kind of focused attention that allows us to see the internal workings of our own minds, be aware of the auto responses of our conditioned minds and gain control over the reactive mind rather than being overwhelmed by it. Mindfulness integrates the working of all the individual parts including the mind, brain, inputs received from the environment through sensory organs, the memory of previous experiences, relationships and thereby enables mastery over mind to achieve harmony and well-being. We all can develop mindfulness that leads to peaceful, harmonious, happy and fulfilling lives. All of us can benefit from this practice to become more healthy and happy individuals who obviously share their happiness with others.

The mindfulness of being aware of the ever changing reality of our body and mind and to "let go" without reacting to the feeling in the mind and sensations in the body, with the understanding of impermanence results in gaining freedom from reacting to our conditioned subconscious mind. This helps us in gaining mastery over our mind, exercise free will and do the right thing by responding rather than reacting to the situation. We can be more focused, experience inner calm and become more joyful, happier and creative.

You and me are a miracle in the flow of life!

Appendix

How does the body produce energy?

All parts of the body need energy to work and this energy comes from the food we eat. It happens due to some sequential biochemical phenomenon known as metabolism. Metabolism provides energy required to sustain life through a sequence of biochemical reactions that take place in trillions of cells of our body. When we eat food, the digestive system produces the nutrients which are absorbed by the cells. The metabolism of these nutrients yields energy and also contributes to the enzyme activity that supports metabolic reactions in the cell.

Metabolic reactions that take place within your body can be categorized as anabolic and catabolic reactions. Anabolism involves production of metabolism precursors such as amino acids, monosaccharides and nucleotides, their activation into reactive forms using energy from ATP, and finally the assembly of these precursors into proteins, polysaccharides, lipids and nucleic

acids. Anabolic processes lead to build up of organs and tissues through growth and differentiation of cells. Examples of anabolic processes include the growth and mineralization of bone and increase in the muscle mass. Anabolic reactions use up energy and are called endergonic reactions. The combining of amino acids to make dipeptides and combining of sugar molecules to become disaccharides are such examples.

Catabolism involves break down of molecules into smaller units and there by release energy. In catabolism, polysaccharides, fat, nucleic acids and proteins are broken down into smaller units such as monosaccharides, fatty acids, nucleotides and amino acids respectively. The purpose of the catabolic reactions is to provide energy. A simple example that occurs in cells is the decomposition of hydrogen peroxide into water and oxygen. The conversion of glucose during respiration to produce carbon dioxide and water is another common example. Thus, the large organic molecules are digested into their smaller components in the cells releasing the energy that is stored.

Thus, anabolic reactions consume energy to combine different molecules where as catabolic reactions release energy while splitting molecules apart. The energy stored in ATP created by catabolic reactions is the fuel for anabolic reactions which synthesize hormones, enzymes, sugars and other substances for cell growth, reproduction, and tissue repair.

The endocrine system stimulates reactions of metabolism by releasing hormones like cortisol, glucagon and adrenaline; digestive system provides nutrients; cardio vascular system transports nutrients through blood; respiratory system provides oxygen and excretory system eliminates waste. Each and every cell in the human body requires energy in order to function. Glucose is the body's primary energy source which is a simple sugar resulting from the digestion of foods containing carbohydrates. Glucose from the digested food circulates in the blood as a ready energy source for all or any cells that need it. Pancreas produces a hormone named insulin. Insulin bonds to a receptor site on the outside of the cell and acts like a key to open a door way into the cell through which glucose can enter.

Some of the glucose can be concentrated as energy sources like glycogen or fatty acids and saved for later use. When insulin production is not adequate, glucose stays in the blood rather than entering the cells. This causes diabetes, the condition in which the pancreas no longer produces enough insulin. Cells may stop responding to the insulin that is produced and as a result, glucose in the blood is not absorbed into the cells of the body and leads to a serious medical condition known as hyperglycemia. Thus, malfunctioning of single hormone "insulin" disturbs the complete metabolism of the body. So this important function in maintaining life, can happen only with perfect coordination of all other systems in the body.

How does the body maintain internal balance?

Homeostasis refers to conditions of stability, balance or equilibrium in the internal environment of the body. The system as a whole regulates its internal environment and maintains a stable condition required for the body to function effectively so that you survive. The nervous and endocrine systems control regulation of body temperature, blood pressure, pH of blood, blood glucose concentration, breathing rate and many other parameters. Secretion of appropriate hormones at the right time by pituitary, thyroid and adrenal glands is just one of the ways the body regulates the temperature as well as blood pressure. Blood pressure is maintained with the active coordination and regulation by each and every one of the organs including brain, lungs, heart and kidneys. Each individual system works in conjunction with other systems to improve our chances of survival by maintaining a stable internal body environment.

Homeostatic mechanisms are dynamic and regulate many different parameters in the human body (e.g., pH, dissolved oxygen, glucose concentration). From the earliest days of physiology – at least as early as the time of Aristotle – physicians recognized that good health was somehow associated with a balance among the multiple life-sustaining forces in the body. The human body is composed of trillions of cells, each of which is packaged to permit movement of certain substances, but not others, across the cell membrane.

The interstitial fluid, with water and solutes, such as ions and gases, moves back and forth between the cell interiors and the blood in nearby capillaries. The activities of cells, tissues and organs must be regulated and integrated with each other so that any change in the extracellular fluid initiates a reaction to correct the change. The compensating mechanisms that mediate such responses are performed by homeostatic control systems.

Positive feedback mechanisms

Positive feedback is the body's mechanism to enhance an output created by a stimulus that is already activated. One such event in the body is release of oxytocin to intensify the contractions that take place during childbirth. The secretion of pepsin, an enzyme that digests proteins is another example. Positive feedback also helps in blood clotting by speeding up the production of thrombin.

Negative feedback mechanisms

Negative feedback mechanisms consist of reducing the output or activity of any organ or system back to its normal range of functioning. Regulation of blood pressure is a good example. The blood vessels act as receptors that sense increase in blood pressure (BP) and relay this message to the brain. The brain then sends a message to the heart and blood vessels. The heart rate would decrease as the blood vessels dilate with increase in diameter and this change would cause the blood pressure to fall back to its normal range. When the BP decreases, vasoconstriction (decrease in diameter of blood vessels) would cause the BP to become normal.

When people reduce food intake while trying to lose weight, the body would reset the metabolic set point to a lower than normal value, which allows the body to continue to function, at a slower rate. The body adjusts itself to a lower metabolic set point to allow the body to survive with relatively low supply of energy. Exercise, however increases the metabolic rate.

Maintenance of body temperature in a certain range is another good example of negative feedback mechanism. The hypothalamus monitors the body temperature and is capable of determining even the slightest variation of normal body temperature (37^0C). Sweating to reduce temperature or shivering to increase body temperature are some of the responses.

What can go wrong?

Homeostatic imbalance results in an unstable internal environment that increases the risk for illness. Nominal negative feedback mechanisms become overwhelmed and destructive positive feedback mechanisms then take over. Diseases that result from a homeostatic imbalance include diabetes, dehydration, hypoglycemia and any disease caused by a toxin present in the blood. Medical intervention is helpful in restoring the balance and preventing damage to the organs.

Thus, many aspects of our body's internal environment e.g. body temperature, the concentration of glucose in the blood, tissue fluid, the osmotic concentration and volume of the blood, are kept at almost constant levels. Thus homeostasis ensures that the body cells are provided with a relatively constant environment, so that they work efficiently and optimally, even though there might be changes outside the body.

Hormones keep the body well coordinated

The wonder of cells is that they see to it that nothing goes wrong by constantly sending and monitoring streams of messages. Most of these signals arrive by means of "couriers" called hormones. The hormones such as insulin, adrenaline, dopamine, estrogen, leptin, oxytocin, renin, cortisol convey information from thyroid and endocrine glands. Messages also arrive from the brain or from regional centers. Cells communicate with their neighbors to make sure their actions are coordinated. Trillions upon trillions of reflexive chemical reactions add up to a mobile, thinking, decision making and hence you are a wonder of "atomic engineering".

The formation of milk after pregnancy called lactation provided by the mother's hormones is one of the best examples of hormonal coordination. It is associated basically to a hormone called "prolactin" produced by the anterior pituitary gland in the brain. During pregnancy the hormones progesterone and estrogen prevent prolactin from being activated and producing milk. But when placenta discharges after pregnancy, prolactin comes into action and contributes to the formation of milk. In different stages of human creation all those things that happen complement one another. Because of this coordination and communication among the hormones, such an important nutrient as mother's milk is prepared exactly at the moment when the baby needs it. The protection that mother's milk provides for the baby from infections is very important for the first few months.

Dopamine is a special neurotransmitter because it is considered to be both excitatory and inhibitory. Dopamine which controls communication in the brain is helpful in overcoming depression and enhances focus. It activates neurons and plays a vital role in functions such as memory, pleasurable reward, behavior, attention, cognition, sleep, mood and learning. Excess and deficiency of this vital chemical is the cause of several disease conditions.

Dopamine problems are implicated in ADHD (Attention deficit hyperactivity disorder), Alzheimer's, Parkinson's, depression, bipolar disorders, schizophrenia etc.

Serotonin is an inhibitory neuro-transmitter which is important for a stable mood and to balance any excessive excitatory (stimulating) neurotransmitters. It regulates sleep cycle, pain control, carbohydrate cravings, and appropriate digestion. Low serotonin levels affect immune system function also. Serotonin is produced by a particular type of neurons in the brain stem and low serotonin levels lead to various forms of depression.

Epinephrine, an excitatory neu-rotransmitter more commonly known as adrenaline, is secreted by the adrenal glands. Epinephrine is released when we experience emotions such as fear or anger causing "Fight-or-Flight Response". It causes an increase in heart rate, blood pressure, and sugar metabolism, preparing the body for strenuous activity. Epinephrine is used as a stimulant in cardiac arrest.

It is also used as a bronchodilator in bronchial asthma. Epinephrine is essential for maintaining cardiovascular homeostasis because of its ability to divert blood to tissues under stress. It increases the coronary artery pressure which results in increased blood flow in coronary arteries.

Leptin and ghrelin are two important hormones that have been identified to have a major influence on energy balance. Leptin is intricately involved in the regulation of appetite, metabolism and calorie burning. Leptin signals the brain about conditions of appetite, creation and use of energy which triggers response from hypothalamus and the thyroid gland. The thyroid gland affects the way our body stores and uses energy. Ghrelin is a fast-acting hormone which stimulates appetite. Sleep also plays an important role in managing the body weight because lack of sleep triggers the body to produce ghrelin, which stimulates hunger. When we get enough sleep, our body will produce another hormone leptin, which suppresses our appetite. In addition, lack of sleep can affect how our body tolerates glucose (blood sugar) and how our body stores energy from food.

The way the brain responds to its hormones indicates that the brain is very adaptable and capable of responding to environmental signals. The brain consists of receptors for thyroid hormones and the six classes of steroid hormones – androgens, estrogens, progestins, glucocorticoids, mineralocorticoids, and vitamin D (all are synthesized from cholesterol). The receptors are present in the selected portions of neurons in the brain and relevant organs in the body. Thyroid and steroid hormones bind to these specific receptor proteins that in turn bind to DNA and regulate the action of genes.

In response to stress and changes in our biological clocks and changes in environment, hormones enter the blood and travel to the brain and other organs. They alter the production of gene products and affect the structure of brain cells as well. The brain adjusts its performance and control of behavior in response to a changing environment. Thus, hormones are important agents of protection and adaptation.

Proteins

Proteins are the "work-horses" of all living systems; as many as a hundred million of them may be busy in any cell at any moment, each unique and each, as far as we know, vital to the maintenance of a sound and happy you. Proteins are what you get when you string amino acids together and we need a lot of them. Each one of them is a little miracle: as to make a protein we need to assemble amino acids not only in the right sequence but they must engage in a "chemical origami" and fold itself into a very specific shape. We need DNA to make proteins and both of them including other components of life could not prosper without some sort of membrane to contain them. These diverse materials can take part in the amazing dance that we call life within the nurturing refuge of a cell.

Amino acids

These are the basic structural building units of proteins. Just as the letters of the alphabet can be combined to form words, a huge variety of proteins are formed by linking amino acids in varied sequences. Twenty standard amino acids are used by cells in protein synthesis, which are synthesized from other molecules. Amino acids are molecules that contain both amine and carboxyl functional groups. The sequence of amino acids in a protein is defined by a gene and encoded in the genetic code.

As amine and carboxylic acid groups of amino acids react to form amide bonds, amino acid molecule can react with another and combine through an amide linkage and this polymerization of amino acids creates proteins. The 20 standard amino acids are either used to synthesize proteins and other bio-molecules or oxidized to urea and carbon dioxide as a source of energy. Hundreds of types of non-protein amino acids have been found in nature and they have multiple functions in living organisms. For example, glycine, gamma-amino butyric acid, and glutamate are neurotransmitters and the thyroid hormones are also alpha-amino acids.

There are 10 essential amino acids, however, which must be obtained from food as the human body cannot synthesize them from other compounds at the level needed for normal growth. Phenylalanine, valine, threonine, tryptophan, isoleucine, methionine, histidine, arginine, leucine and lysine are essential amino acids. A common mnemonic evolved for remembering them is PVT TIM HALL using the first letter of each of these amino acids. These ten valuable amino acids have long preserved life in humans. Amino acids can be obtained through the consumption of foods containing proteins which are broken down through digestion by enzymes called proteases.

As the physicist Paul Davies puts it 'If everything needs everything else, how did the community of molecules ever arise in the first place?' It is rather as if all the ingredients in your kitchen somehow got together and baked themselves into a cake – a cake that could moreover divide when necessary to produce more cakes. It is little wonder that we call it the miracle of life!

Functions of protein

Proteins are involved in virtually all cell functions. Some proteins provide structural support and some of them provide defense against germs. Antibodies are specialized proteins which are involved in defending the body from antigens by immobilizing them so that they can be destroyed by white blood cells.

Contractile proteins such as actin and myosin are responsible for muscle contraction and movement. The structure and function of contractile proteins in striated muscles is well characterized and provides a good example for extrapolation to an analysis of contractile protein structure and function in non-muscle cells. However, the interaction of contractile proteins of various cells may be unique.

Enzymes such as lactase and pepsin are proteins that facilitate and speed up chemical reactions. Lactase breaks down the sugar lactose found in milk and Pepsin is a digestive enzyme that works in the stomach to break down proteins in food.

Hormonal proteins such as insulin, oxytocin, and somatotropin are messenger proteins. Insulin regulates glucose metabolism by controlling the blood-sugar concentration. Oxytocin stimulates contractions in females during childbirth. Somatotropin is a growth hormone that stimulates protein production in muscle cells.

Structural proteins such as collagen and elastin are fibrous and stringy and provide support for connective tissues such as tendons and ligaments. Storage proteins store amino acids. Ovalbumin is found in egg whites and casein is a milk-based protein. Transport proteins such as hemoglobin and cytochromes which move different types of molecules through the body. Hemoglobin transports oxygen through the blood and Cytochromes are electron carrier proteins.

A cell makes proteins by joining together amino acids into long chains and in the right order, a phenomenon known as protein synthesis. As they are made, the chains begin to take on their complex shapes. First, it makes a copy of the relevant DNA instruction in the cell nucleus, and takes it into the cytoplasm. Once in the cytoplasm, the mRNA is snatched up by tiny protein-assembly machines called ribosomes. Each ribosome reads the code from 'start' to 'stop', selects the correct amino acid building blocks and ejects growing protein. A cell can assemble a small protein like insulin in just a few seconds.

Enzymes

Enzymes are incredibly efficient and highly specific catalysts. There are approximately 1300 different enzymes found in the human cell and all the 100 trillion cells in our body depend upon the reactions of metabolic enzymes and their energy factor. The human body speeds the overall reaction through a series of enzyme-mediated steps –Amylase breaks down starch, lipase breaks down fats, protease breaks proteins, cellulose breaks down fiber, lactase breaks down milk and so on.

Metabolic enzymes: Metabolic enzymes are useful for detoxification and energy production and without them cellular life would cease to exist. An important metabolic enzyme is superoxide dismutase (SOD) which is an antioxidant that protects the cells by attacking free radicals. To perform each step in glycolysis phenomenon, our body relies on different kinds of enzymes. Thus, to get energy from glucose, our body must carry out a series of chemical reactions in a predetermined order to yield an essential fuel called adenosine triphosphate, or ATP, which powers most of our cells in the body.

Digestive Enzymes: Digestive enzymes are secreted along the digestive tract to break food down into nutrients and waste. Pancreas produces most of the digestive enzymes which are involved in absorption of nutrients into the blood stream. Some human digestive enzymes include proteases (pepsin, trypsin and chymotrypsin), amylase, lipase and ptyalin etc.

Proteases

Any enzyme that breaks down protein into its building blocks, amino acids, is called a protease. Pepsin, trypsin and chymotrypsin are the enzymes produced by the digestive tract. Pepsin breaks down proteins into peptides and begins protein digestion. Pancreas makes trypsin and chymotrypsin enzymes that are released into the small intestine through the pancreatic duct. Trypsin and chymotrypsin complete protein digestion while producing amino acids that are absorbed into blood.

Amylase

It is another digestive enzyme that acts by breaking down starch when we chew our food, converting it into maltose, a smaller carbohydrate. Cells in our pancreas make pancreatic amylase, which acts as a catalyst in digestion of carbohydrate, producing glucose, which is absorbed into our blood and carried throughout our body.

Lipase

It is an enzyme that breaks down dietary fats into smaller molecules called fatty acids and glycerol. A minute amount of lipase, called gastric lipase, is made by cells in our stomach. This enzyme specifically digests butter fat in food. The main source of lipase in the digestive tract is pancreas, which makes pancreatic lipase that acts in our small intestine. First, bile made in the liver and released into the intestine converts dietary fat into fatty acids and glycerol, which travel in blood and lymph vessels to reach all parts of the body.

Although protease, amylase and lipase are the three major enzymes that help in digestion, other enzymes like maltase, sucrose and lactase present in the lining of intestine are also capable to convert a specific type of sugar into glucose. Renin acts on proteins in milk and gelatinase digests gelatin and collagen. Ptyalin is another enzyme that is part of our saliva and aids with digestion. Ptyalin helps digestion by breaking down starches and glycogens as they enter our mouth. After the starches and glycogen are mixed with saliva, they are broken down into maltose and glucose – simple sugars that can be used more readily by the body.

Enzymes involved in DNA copying

Enzymes are also involved in DNA replication and protein synthesis. DNA helicase is an enzyme, which unwinds the DNA strands from their normal helix shape or configuration, and DNA polymerase III activates the copying process. DNA ligase is a specific type of enzyme that facilitates the joining of DNA strands together by catalyzing the formation of a phosphodiester bond during DNA replication. It plays a role in repairing single-strand breaks in duplex DNA. Primase is an enzyme that synthesizes short RNA sequences (called primers) which serve as a starting point for DNA synthesis.

Enzymes play a critical role in everyday life. When levels of certain enzymes are low or absent (called an "enzyme deficiency") the body may not function normally. Many heritable genetic disorders such as diabetes, Tay-Sachs disease occur because there is a deficiency or total absence of one or more enzymes.

Neurons

Neurons are the most significant cells of the brain which respond to stimulus and communicate the presence of that stimulus to the central nervous system. Neurons communicate with one another by sending messages back and forth in the form of electrochemical signals or impulses. The nerve cells are organized in networks or patterns that shape individual behavior and make each one of us unique in our own way. The DNA in our nerve cells is almost the same as DNA in other cells of the body with the exception of red blood cells which do not have DNA.

The brain contains about 100 billion neurons and each one of them is a fraction of a millimeter in size. Sensory neurons send signals to the spinal cord and brain responding to stimuli such as light, sound and touch. Motor neurons receive signals from the brain and spinal cord and cause muscle contractions. Interneurons connect neurons to other neurons within the brain and spinal cord.

The structure of nerve cells is different from other cells. Neuron is like a tree with a trunk, roots, branches and twigs. The trunk of the tree is a long fiber called an axon with root like ends called synaptic terminals. The dendrites that are similar to branches and twigs are flexible antenna like extensions. Dendrites terminate in tiny, granular knob like bumps called dendrite spines which receive information. Neurons communicate through their axons and dendrites through intricate patterns of networks. The axon sends electrochemical information to other neurons and the dendrites receive messages from other neurons.

The cell body of neuron contains a well-defined nucleus, surrounded by granular cytoplasm. It has all the cell organelles like other cells but centrosome is absent because nerve cells have lost the ability to divide. The ability of neurons to receive and transmit information depends on their elaborate structure with extensions of the cell called dendrites and axons.

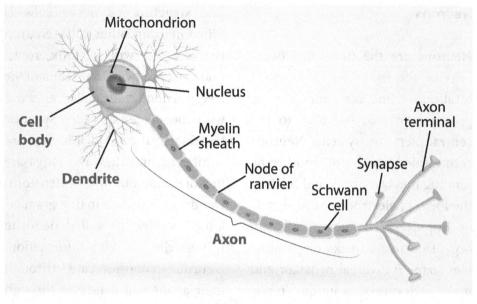

Structure of Neuron

Structure of a neuron: Axon is typically a much longer extension that transmits signals to other cells, which may be effector cells or neurons. The conical region of an axon where it joins the cell body is called the axon hillock, where the signals that travel down the axon are generated. Myelin sheath encloses the axons which are further divided into several branches. The end of the axon is called synaptic terminal and the communication between a synaptic terminal and another cell is called a synapse. Information is passed from the transmitting neuron (the presynaptic cell) to the receiving cell (the postsynaptic cell) by means of chemical messengers called neurotransmitters. The complexity of a neuron's shape reflects the number of synapses it has with other neurons and a single interneuron can have as many as 100,000 synapses on its highly branched dendrites.

Glia: Glia are supporting cells that are essential for the structural integrity of the nervous system and for the normal functioning of neurons. There are several types of glia in the brain and spinal cord, including astrocytes, radial glia, oligodendrocytes and Schwann cells. The term "astrocyte" refers to the star-like shape of the cells, which provide structural support for neurons and regulate the extracellular concentrations of ions and neurotransmitters. The radial glial cells exclusively serve as a passive scaffold for cell migration. Oligodendrocytes in the CNS and Schwann cells in the PNS are glia that forms the myelin sheaths around the axons of many vertebrate neurons. Microglia normally ingests cell debris and bacteria as part of the body's immune response. Schwann cells wrap themselves around axons in PNS, forming layers of myelin which provides electrical insulation of the axon.

Nerves: A nerve is an enclosed, cable-like bundle of axons in the peripheral nervous system. The electrochemical nerve impulses are transmitted along each of the axons bundled in a nerve to peripheral organs. A nerve is formed of a bundle of nerve fibers (axons) enclosed in a tubular sheath. It may be compared to an underground electric cable containing numerous conducting wires each insulated from the other. The myelin sheath of the axon acts like an insulation and prevents mixing of impulses in the adjacent axons.

Nerves can be categorized as Spinal nerves (which innervate much of the body and connect through the spinal column to the spinal cord) and Cranial nerves (that innervate parts of the head and connect directly to the brain especially to the brainstem).

Messaging: Ions are charged atoms which generate electrical signals for communication between neurons. A neuron's cell membrane which is about 8 nanometers thick allows certain ions to diffuse through it, but restricts other ions. The ions which play a significant role in polarizing and depolarizing the cell are sodium, potassium and chloride ions. When a neuron is in resting state the inner surface of its cell membrane has a negative charge relative to its surroundings and when a neuron is activated more ions instantly move into the neuron through the cell membrane, making the inner surface change from a negative charge to positive charge. This flow of ions, which lasts for only a few milliseconds, propagates an electric current called action potential that travels down the axon. When a nerve cell reaches a certain threshold of electrical charge, flow of electrical charges takes place along its membrane to the axon terminals and after that reverts back to its resting state. When the stimulus is strong enough to cause a nerve cell to turn on or fire, it generates a self propagating electrical impulse which goes all the way down to the end of axon. The electric current flows down the axon to its terminals in an all-or-none phenomena. The all-or-none law is the principle by which a nerve or muscle fiber responds to a stimulus independent of the strength of the stimulus. The nerve or muscle fiber responds if stimulus exceeds the threshold potential; otherwise, there is no response.

Ion Channels: Ion channels are pore-forming proteins which are present on all membranes of cells as well as intracellular organelles (nucleus, mitochondria, endoplasmic reticulum, golgi apparatus and so on). The electrochemical gradient across the membrane controls the voltage gradient across the plasma membrane of cells by regulating the flow across the membrane. In some ion channels, passage through the pore is governed by a "gate," which may be opened or closed by chemical or electrical signals. Cells are electrically polarized as they maintain a voltage difference across the cell's plasma membrane, known as the membrane potential. Electrical polarization occurs due to complex interplay between protein structures embedded in the membrane called ion pumps and ion channels.

Gated ion channels are responsible for generating the signals of the nervous system. The membrane potential may change in response to stimuli that open or close those gated ion channels. Some such stimuli trigger a hyper polarization, an increase in the magnitude of the membrane potential. Depolarization is nothing but a reduction in the magnitude of membrane potential which is triggered by some other stimuli.

In neurons, the types of ion channels in the membrane usually vary across different parts of the cell. The dendrites, axon, and cell body have different electrical properties. So some parts of the membrane of a neuron may be excitable (capable of generating action potentials), whereas others are not. Axon hillock (the point where the axon leaves the cell body) is usually the most excitable part of a neuron. The axon and cell body are also excitable in most cases.

Stretch-gated ion channels respond when cells sense stretch. The channels are opened when the membrane is mechanically deformed. Ligand-gated ion channels, which are found at synapses, open or close when a neurotransmitter flows to the channel. Voltage-gated ion channels in axons open or close when the membrane potential changes.

Action Potentials: Action potentials are the signals that carry information along axons, sometimes over great distances, such as from toes to spinal cord. It is a short-lasting event in which the electrical membrane potential of a cell rapidly rises and falls. Action potentials are generated by voltage-gated sodium and calcium channels. The former last for less than one millisecond while the latter may last for 100 milliseconds or longer.

In a myelinated axon, voltage-gated Na^+ and K^+ channels are concentrated at gaps in the myelin sheath called Nodes of Ranvier. Action potentials are not generated in the regions between the nodes as the extracellular fluid is in contact with the axon membrane only at the nodes. The inward current produced during the rising phase of the action potential at a node travels all the way to the next node. A new action potential is generrarted at that node. The action potential jumps along the axon from node to node. Saltatory (leap) conduction is the propagation of action potentials along myelinated axons from one node of Ranvier to the next node. It travels at speeds up to 120 m/sec in myelinated axons as there is increase in the conduction velocity of action potentials without corresponding increase the diameter of an axon. Electrical synapses however allow electrical current to flow directly from cell to cell at gap junctions.

Synapses: There is a space between neurons which is about one millionth of a centimeter in width called the synapse. Neurons communicate with other cells at synapses. A vast majority of synapses are chemical synapses. The presynaptic neuron releases a neurotransmitter which is synthesized and packaged in its synaptic vesicles. Hundreds of synaptic terminals may interact with the cell body and dendrites of a postsynaptic neuron. When an action potential reaches a synaptic terminal, it depolarizes the terminal membrane, causing some of the synaptic vesicles to release the neurotransmitter. Synaptic cleft is the narrow gap between presynaptic neuron and post synaptic neuron. Neurotransmitter diffuses across the synaptic cleft and a variety of factors can affect the amount of neurotransmitter that is released. The responsiveness of the postsynaptic cell also depends on various factors and forms the basis for learning and memory.

Chemical synapses are specialized junctions through which cells of the nervous system signal to one another and to non-neuronal cells. They allow the neurons of the central nervous system to form interconnected neural circuits. At many chemical synapses, ligand-gated ion channels capable of binding to the neurotransmitter are clustered in the membrane of the postsynaptic cell, directly opposite to the synaptic terminal. Binding of the neurotransmitter to a particular part of the channel, the receptor, opens the channel and allows specific ions to diffuse across the postsynaptic membrane. This mechanism of information transfer is called direct synaptic transmission. The result is generally a postsynaptic potential, a change in the membrane potential of the postsynaptic cell. Unlike action potentials, which are all-or-none, postsynaptic potentials are graded as their magnitude varies depending on the amount of neurotransmitter released by the presynaptic neuron and other factors. Another difference is that postsynaptic potentials usually do not regenerate themselves as they spread along the membrane of a cell; they become smaller with distance from the synapse.

The interplay between excitatory and inhibitory inputs from multiple neurons is the essence of integration in the nervous system. The axon hillock is the neuron's integrating center and the membrane potential at any instant represents the summed effect of all EPSPs (Excitatory Postsynaptic Potential) and IPSPs (Inhibitory Postsynaptic Potential). Action potential is generated when the membrane potential at the axon hillock reaches the threshold. Action potential then travels along the axon to its synaptic terminals. After the refractory period, the neuron may produce another action potential if the threshold is reached again at the axon hillock. On the other hand, the summed effect of EPSP and IPSP may hold the membrane potential below the threshold, preventing production of action potentials.

Neurotransmitters: Neurotransmitters are the chemicals which allow the transmission of signals from one neuron to the next across synapses. A few important neurotransmitter actions are Glutamate, GABA, Acetylcholine, Dopamine and Serotonin. Neurotransmitters are synthesized by nerve cells, actively transported along the axons and stored in the synaptic vesicles. They are released by exocytosis (a process by which the contents of a cell vacuole are released to the exterior through fusion of the vacuole membrane with the cell membrane) in response to the action potential and diffuse across the synaptic cleft.

- Armand Delsemme - *Our Cosmic Universe*

- Bill Bryson - *A Short History of Nearly Everything*

- Bob Wallace, Jerry Sanders, Rob Ferl - *Biology - The Science of Life*

- Campbell, Reece - *Biology*

- Carl Sagan - *Billions and Billions*

- Carl Sagan - *Cosmos*

- David Eagleman - *Incognito: The Secret Lives of the Brain*

- Fritjof Capra - *The Tao of Physics*

- Gary William Flake - *The Computational Beauty of Nature*

- Gary Zukav - *The Dancing Wu Li Masters*

- Hermann Hesse - *Siddhartha*

- Joanne Baker - *50 quantum physics ideas you really need to know*

- Joe Dispenza, D.C - *Evolve Your Brain*

- John Gribbin - *Almost Everyone's Guide to Science*

- John Gribbin - *In search of Schrodinger's Cat Quantum Physics and Reality*

- Joseph Silk - *On the Shores of the Unknown*

- Kim E. Barrett, Susan M. Barman, Scott Boitano, Heddwen L. Brooks - *Ganong's Review of Medical Physiology*

- Martin Gardner - *Great Essays in Science*

- Martin Rees - *Just Six Numbers*

- Michael Guillen - *Five Equations That Changed the World*

- Richard P. Feynman - *The Pleasure of Finding Things Out*

- S.N. Goenka - *The Art of Living*

- Stephen Hawking - *A Brief History of Time*

- Stephen Hawking - *The Universe in a Nutshell*

- Sylvia S. Mader - *Biology*

♦ Charles Darwin, *On The Origin of Species By Means of Natural Selection*, London. John Murray, 1859.

♦ de Duve, Christian. *A Guided Tour of the Living Cell. 2 vols.* New York: Scientific American/Rockefeller University Press, 1984.

♦ Eric S. Lander, Professor of Biology; Professor of Systems Biology, Harvard Medical School; Founding Director, the Broad Institute of MIT and Harvard PhD, 1981 Oxford University – said in an interview given for Academy of achievement in June 19, 1999.

♦ Feynman, Richard P. *Mathematical Formulation of the Quantum Theory of Electromagnetic Interaction*, in Schwinger, J. (ed.), Selected Papers of Quantum Electrodynamics, New York, Dover, 1958, p. 272ff.

♦ Feynman, Richard P. *Six Easy Pieces*. London: Penguin Books, 1998.

♦ Ford, K. *The world of Elementary Particles*. New York, Blaisdell, 1963.

♦ Fortey, Richard. *Life: An Unauthorised Biography*. London: Flamingo/HarperCollins, 1998.

♦ Haldane, J.B.S. *Adventures of a Biologist*. New York: Harper & Brothers, 1937. What is Life? New York: Boni and Gaer, 1947.

♦ Lawrence Joseph Henderson, *The Fitness of environment*, Nabu Press, 1913, 2010.

- Lynn Margulis and Dorion Sagan, *What is Life?*, California: University of California Press, 2000.

- Oparin Aleksandr and Haldane, *Origin Of Life: Twentieth Century Landmarks*, Chris Gordon-Smith, 2003.

- Rees, Martin. *Just Six Numbers: The Deep Forces That Shape the Universe*, New York: Basic Books, 2001.

- Sagan, Carl. *Cosmos*. New York: Ballantine Books, 1980.

- Walter J Freeman, *Consciousness, Intentionality, and Causality*, Journal of Consciousness Studies 6 Nov/Dec: 143-172, 1999.

- *www.wonderwhizkids.com*

Adenoids are the mass of lymphoid tissue in the upper part of throat behind the nose. They help to defend the body from infection. They trap bacteria and viruses which you breathe in through your nose.

Adenosine triphosphate is a nucleoside triphosphate used in cells as a coenzyme, often called the "molecular unit of currency" of intracellular energy transfer. ATP transports chemical energy within cells for metabolism.

Adipose tissue, or fat, is an anatomical term for loose connective tissue composed of adipocytes. Its main role is to store energy in the form of fat, although it also cushions and insulates the body.

Adrenal glands are endocrine glands that sit at the top of kidneys. They are chiefly responsible for releasing hormones in response to stress through the synthesis of corticosteroids.

Amniotic fluid is a clear, slightly yellowish liquid that surrounds the unborn baby (fetus) during pregnancy. It is contained in the amniotic sac.

Angina is a type of chest pain caused by reduced blood flow to the heart muscle. Angina is a symptom of coronary artery disease. Angina is typically described as squeezing, pressure, heaviness, tightness or pain in the chest.

Anoxia is a condition characterized by an absence of oxygen supply to an organ or a tissue.

Apoptosis is the process of programmed cell death (PCD) that may occur in multicellular organisms. Biochemical events lead to characteristic cell changes (morphology) and death.

Archaea constitute a domain or kingdom of single-celled microorganisms. These microbes are prokaryotes, meaning that they have no cell nucleus or any other membrane-bound organelles in their cells.

Big bang is the rapid expansion of matter from a state of extremely high density and temperature which according to current cosmological theories marked the origin of the Universe.

Cell differentiation is the process by which a less specialized cell becomes a more specialized cell type. Differentiation occurs numerous times during the development of a multicellular organism as the organism changes from a simple zygote to a complex system of tissues and cell types and an individual.

Complementary strand of DNA or RNA may be constructed based on nucleobase complementarity. Each base pair, A=T vs. G≡C, takes up roughly the same space, thereby enabling a twisted DNA double helix formation without any special distortions.

Cyanobacteria or blue-green algae are aquatic and photosynthetic, that is, they live in the water, and can manufacture their own food. Because they are bacteria, they are quite small and usually unicellular, though they often grow in colonies large enough to see.

Cytokines are the small proteins released by cells that have a specific effect on the interactions between cells, on communications between cells or on the behavior of cells.

Dark matter is the non-luminous material which is postulated to exist in space and which could take either of two forms: weakly interacting particles (cold dark matter) or high-energy randomly moving particles created soon after the Big Bang (hot dark matter).

Dynamo effect is a geophysical theory that explains the origin of the Earth's main magnetic field in terms of a self-exciting (or self-sustaining) dynamo.

Embryogenesis is the processes leading to the development of an embryo from egg to completion of the embryonic stage.

Endosymbiosis is an evolutionary theory which explains the origin of eukaryotic cells from prokaryotes. It states that several key organelles like mitochondria and plastids of eukaryotes originated as symbiosis between separate single-celled organisms.

Enteric nervous system (ENS) is the intrinsic nervous system of the gastrointestinal tract. It contains complete reflex circuits that detect the physiological condition of the gastrointestinal tract.

Gene flow also called migration—is any movement of genes from one population to another. Migration into or out of a population may be responsible for a marked change in allele frequencies.

Gene knock out technology is a genetic technique in which one of an organism's genes is made inoperative ("knocked out" of the organism). Mice are currently the most closely related laboratory animal species to humans for which the knockout technique can easily be applied.

Genotype is the genetic constitution of an organism based on the alleles present. Genotypes determine which characteristics the individual will express, for example: whether they have freckles or not, if they are lactose intolerant etc.

Histones are a family of basic proteins that associate with DNA in the nucleus and help condense it into chromatin..

Hypoxia or altitude sickness, reduces the amount of oxygen in the brain causing such symptoms as dizziness, shortness of breath, and mental confusion.

Independent assortment is a basic principle of genetics developed by a monk named Gregor Mendel. This principle states that the alleles for a trait separate when gametes are formed. These allele pairs are then randomly united at fertilization.

Junk DNA is that portion of DNA which is not transcribed and expressed, comprising about 90% of the 3 billion base pairs of the human genome; its function is not known.

Macrophages are large, specialized cells that recognize, engulf and destroy target cells. They are important cells of the immune system that are formed in response to an infection or accumulating damaged or dead cells.

Metamorphosis is a biological process by which an animal physically develops after birth or hatching, involving a conspicuous

and relatively abrupt change in the animal's form or structure through cell growth and differentiation.

mRNA is the molecule in cells that carries codes from the DNA in the nucleus to the sites of protein synthesis in the cytoplasm (the ribosomes).

Myogenesis is the formation of muscular tissue, particularly during embryonic development.

Neurogenesis is process by which new nerve cells are generated. In neurogenesis, there is active production of new neurons, astrocytes, glia, and other neural lineages from undifferentiated neural progenitor or stem cells.

Notochord is a flexible rod-like structure that is present in the embryos of all chordates and in the adult forms of certain groups. The notochord develops into the spinal column in most vertebrates.

Nucleosome is a section of DNA that is wrapped around a core of proteins. Inside the nucleus, DNA forms a complex with proteins called chromatin, which allows the DNA to be condensed into a smaller volume.

Phagocytes are the white blood cells that protect the body by eating dirt, bacteria and dead or dying cells. They are important for fighting infections. They are also important for becoming immune.

Phenotype is all the observable characteristics of an organism, such as shape, size, color, and behavior that result from the interaction of its genotype (total genetic inheritance) with the environment.

Phytoremediation is fixing environmental problems through the use of plants. Some plants absorb copper compounds through their roots. They concentrate these compounds as a result of this. The plants can be burned to produce an ash that contains the copper compounds.

Pituitary gland is an important gland in the body and it is often referred to as the 'master gland', because it controls several of the other hormone glands (e.g. adrenals, thyroid).

Placenta is an organ that connects the developing fetus to the uterine wall to allow nutrient uptake, waste elimination, and gas exchange via the mother's blood supply, fights against internal infection and produces hormones to support pregnancy.

Protobionts are systems that are considered to have possibly been the precursors to prokaryotic cells.

Recombination is the rearrangement of genetic material, especially by crossing over in chromosomes or by the artificial joining of segments of DNA from different organisms to create genetic diversity.

RNA world hypothesis proposes that a world filled with life based on ribonucleic acid (RNA) predates the current world of life based on deoxyribonucleic acid (DNA) and protein.

Somatic cell nuclear transfer is a laboratory technique for creating a viable embryo from a body cell and an egg cell. The technique consists of taking an enucleated oocyte (egg cell) and implanting a donor nucleus from a somatic (body) cell.

SRY gene is a gene for maleness found on the Y chromosome. It has a key role in development of the testes and determination of sex.

Stromatolites are layered bio-chemical structures formed in shallow water by the trapping, binding and cementation of sedimentary grains by biofilms of microorganisms, especially cyanobacteria.

Transcription is the process by which the information in a strand of DNA is copied into a new molecule of messenger RNA (mRNA).

Transcription factors are proteins involved in the process of converting, or transcribing, DNA into RNA.

Transgenic animal is one whose genome has been changed to carry genes from other species. Examples: Dolly sheep, Glofish etc.

Umbilical cord is the cord that connects the developing fetus with the placenta while the fetus is in the uterus. The umbilical cord is clamped and cut at birth, and its residual tip forms the bellybutton.

Vernix is a white, cheesy substance that covers and protects the skin of a fetus. Vernix is still all over the skin of a baby at birth. Vernix is composed of sebum (skin oil) and cells that have sloughed off the skin of the fetus.